CITY BOY

TO

TIMBER BEAST

CITY BOY

TO

TIMBER BEAST

Memoirs of my journey from the city

to the U.S. Forest Service

DALE X PHIPPS

DEDICATION

To my father, Oliver Phipps who believed in me. I knew he was smart and became even smarter as I grew older.

To James Blackman, MD who saved my life in 1947 when no other doctors could.

City Boy to Timber Beast

Table of Contents

City Boy to Timber Beast

Prologue

I wrote these short stories for my children to remember me by, and for others to see what work in the forest was like for me. My story really began at age 11, when I joined the Boy Scouts. I attended many spring and winter weekend campouts in my first 4 years of Scouting. Camp Fife, the Yakima Washington area summer camp, was a weeklong outdoor adventure. During my second summer at Camp Fife, I was chosen by my fellow scouts as an outstanding camper and awarded the honor of becoming an Order of Arrow member. Because of this award, and the fact I was an avid archer, I was hired to instruct archery and other outdoor skills at Camp Fife for three summers 1955, 56, 57. In the Fall of 1957 I became an Eagle Scout. In the summer of 1958, I was chosen to work at Philmont Scout Ranch, the Boy Scouts of America's largest National High Adventure Base. National Boy Scout camp, Philmont, located in Cimarron, New Mexico.

With this much stirred up outdoor background, one can only see that when given the opportunity to hire on to the U.S. Forest Service I took it with my eyes wide open. Most of my short stories within this book cover the 35 years of Timber Management as a Timber Sale Officer. After my 35 years of full time Timber management which included other duties as assigned i.e.: fire- fighting, back country patrol, engineering aid, searches for lost people, first aid, Wildlife (Spotted Owl protection), and yes even camp ground clean up after Holidays and at the start of new camping seasons.

Timber Beast: If you are wondering what a Timber Beast is. He or She is a person who works in the Forest Service Timber Department. It's a jovial slang name given to the men and women of the Timber Dept. by the other Departments within the Forest Service.

After my retirement and a few years of play, and odd jobs, I knew I had to go back to the forest, and I found an opportunity for me. In the last 10 years of Sale Administration, I was involved in the finding and the protection of the Endangered Spotted Owl. And in 2003 the Naches District Wildlife crew numbers were shrinking due to budget cuts, so I've volunteered every Spotted Owl protocol season since. This will probably be another book in the future, on my searching for, capturing and banding new and juvenile owls. That's not all -- with 15+ summers of Spotted Owl surveys, a lot of other forest things have happened that I've come across.   TUNE IN.

Chapter 1

My Beginning with the Forest Service

In the first few weeks of 1958, in my senior year of high school at Marquette High, those who were not planning on attending collage were given an aptitude test. The reasoning for the test was to help the seniors search for ideas of what jobs they were knowledgeable enough to work at and would be willing to strive and study for, even maybe an apprenticeship while in school for that kind of work.

About 2 weeks later those who had taken the test were given a field day. Some field day- in an Unemployment office going over our test. There were 10 maybe 12 of us and we were shown job opportunities on slides and short movies of different jobs available in our area. While these motivating job possibilities were being shown to us each student was given individual counseling. The counseling was trying to pair the test we had weeks earlier with things that could be and were available in the Yakima area.

It was sometime in the afternoon that it was my turn to talk and get ideas from a young new counselor. Now bless his heart he did not know quite how to take some of the answers I had given on the test. The one question and my answer that stood out was an old-world type question. It was trying to line you up with the job your father had, a shoemaker, a butcher, a brick layer etc. Well in my youth and boldness it PISSED ME OFF. My answer was my father was a ditch digger I wanted to see how they would pair me up with a job. After the counselor read my answer he did not quite know where I was coming from with that answer. I told him that I did not appreciate that type of question; it was too simple to just match someone up with whatever their father had done to make a living. The counselor agreed that it was a pathetic simple way to avoid the real work to find a young man a job. As it turned out I had a high ranking in math and the counselor said that would be a big loss in a ditch. From then on, we got along quite well. To say the least he kind of took a liking to me and was willing to go the extra effort to help me find that perfect job. We chatted on possibilities and my personal desires. I was just coming off a 3-year relationship that did not end well and my biggest need was to get out of Yakima. I loved the forest. I had worked summers at Camp Fife Boy Scout camp in the Bumping area and just returned from Cimarron New Mexico and the Philmont Scout Ranch. While there I instructed Scouts and their Leaders how to live in the out of doors by hiking, camping, cooking, horsemanship just all outdoors stuff. I told him that I needed any kind of employment he could find me in the forest. He agreed to keep me on his job-hunting list and that there was 9 months till graduation so both our hopes were high.

Well, those 9 months flew by, only 8 months went by and I got a call from the Unemployment Office. My Employment Counselor had come through for me. We had not spoken since the day in September and I had totally forgotten my request for a forest job. His first question to me was had I remembered what I had asked him to search for me? Boy was that a flash back "YES." Suddenly, I remember my request and I still wanted it. His second question was could I get out of school for a few hours this week? He had an appointment set up for me at the Naches Ranger Station (RS) in the afternoon of the following day. Of course, I could get out of school for a couple of hours. I was a senior with less than a month left of school before graduation. The job was for a Clerk (title: Forestry Tech) for 9 to 10 months a year with possible advancement to full employment. I was to meet with the Assistant Ranger and their Log Scaler. I had no idea what a log scale was, but I was willing to learn. (Scaler: one who measures logs)

The interview went well with the FS personnel. They already knew everything about my history from the Unemployment Counselor of Scout camps for four summer jobs 1955, 56, 57, 58 and I was about to graduate with 12 years of Catholic schooling. The top questions to me! 1. Did I know how to operate a 10 key? Yes, I used one at scout camp in the commissary. 2. Could I operate a calculator? (in those days it was a 50# electric monster that needed manual help to do divisions and fractions.

The one they were talking about was one liked what we used in our Business Course our junior year at Marquette. Yes, I knew all about the Marchant Calculator. 3. When could I start work? Because things were backing up in their record keeping department, they need my help as soon as possible. Two weeks later after graduation I was a Scale Clerk working for the Forest Service.

My first job as a scale clerk included a lot of data compiling from log scale tickets. Some days as many as 120 scale tickets to compile volume on. There were 3 scalers at three different log scaling locations. Their job was to take the dimensions of every log on trucks coming from the Naches and Tieton Ranger Districts. They were to write down the length the diameters of both ends and find any deductions for rot or breakage of each log on a scale ticket. Some loads were only 3 or 4 logs while others their where as many as 50 logs per load. At the end of the day the log scale tickets were brought to the Naches Ranger Station where I could start the following day to fill in volumes on all the tickets using the dimensions they recorded. Each day for me ended with a summary of all logs hauled by species, volume, and loads of logs by District and by each different log sale area. At the end of each month there was the compiling of Cutting Reports for each Sale and each Purchaser. I was in fat heaven as I was actually doing things with the math I had been taught in High School and loving the challenge of keeping up with the three scalers and even getting ahead from time to time.

The second year of this first job with the Forest Service was even better. On occasions the assistant Ranger would offer me the chance to go to the field and experience the logging operations firsthand. Then during one of these field trips we happened to pass by some recent blowdown trees. Packy, the assistant Ranger, suggested that we mark the trees for a small sale and sell them through a bid auction. We marked and estimated the volume of the 3 or 4 blowdown and collected information to describe their location in the forest. When we returned to the F.S. station I was instructed on the ins and outs of making a small sale contract and advertising its sale date. Mind you I was still trying to keep up with the scalers and their 100 loads of logs to be processed and recorded cach day. Well, this new experience did not go unnoticed between the Ranger and his assistant. They thought it would be a good idea if in my spare time I could work in small sales. I would do most of the sale paperwork and a Forester would help me in the marking and measurement of dead, dying, or down merchantable tree. The field work (and learning curve) went well since I knew all the tree species from my time in Boy Scouting. All I needed was to pick up on how to make deductions for rot or breakage of a distressed tree. Soon I was totally on my own marking, measuring, compiling the sale data, and selling Small Sales. Most of the small sales were 2 to 5 truckloads of logs, which were approximate 5 thousand board feet per load. My next and almost consecutive new job with the making of small sales was the administration of same. Each sale needed an observer to check on the operator removing the timber, to be sure they were finding all included trees, taking care not to damage other resources such as roads, streams, meadows, live trees nearby, and that the operator was utilizing all the merchantable wood possible from the marked trees. This administrator (observer) was normally a young Forester which was a good use of his or her recent collage experience put to work in the forest. However, when summer arrived and all our Timber Dept. summer help arrived, they became Forman's to a 6-man timber marking crew. And because of that I received one more advancement –Small Sales Administrator-. Somehow things got going so well with preparing, selling and adman and dealing with the Small Sale Loggers that I needed help with the scale tickets, so Norma (first woman to work at Naches Ranger Station) was chosen to come in and help me with the scale and small sales preparation.

Big Bill & Logger with tractor. ©Dale X Phipps

The Big Storm

Around the time of my fourth year at Naches R.S. we had the Columbus Day Storm October12, 1962. The storm winds blew down thousands of trees in the upper Bumping River drainage, mainly along the Deep Creek road starting at the Twin Sisters trail head and down approximately 3 miles to the Deep Creek Bridge. The blow down besides being 3 miles long it was also about ½ mile wide. This kind of upended all Naches R.D. forest plans. Our directions from the Regional Office in Portland were to start immediately cruising, mapping and planning with total consideration of its location which was adjacent to the *Cougar Lake Wilderness. The removal of all trees blown down was to avoid any possible bug infestations brought on from all this new down and dying timber. By midsummer 1963 the blow down trees were advertised and sold to Boise Cascade Lumber Co. It was called the Copper City Blow down Sale. Besides the tree removal special requirements were made to protect the remaining area by requiring all skidding tractors (tractors that pull logs from the forest to a log loading area) to be no larger than a D-6 and no blades on the tractors. Without blades they would make a narrow path and damage fewer standing trees. As it turned out I was given my first big sale to administer because all the Foresters were running marking crews, planting crews, or on firefighting standby.

Cougar Lake Wilderness was an area set aside by the Forest Service to be un-touched by man's activity. Except in times of a disaster, but only then everything must be considered by being as gentle as possible not to disturb natural features and vegetation. This area is now part of the William O Douglas Wilderness.

As it turned out even though the Forest Service had made many efforts in the planning and sale contract to protect the environment there were those who believed that no logging should occur. They did not understand that if a fire were to start in all that downfall it would grow so fast that millions of additional trees could be lost, nor did they understand that large numbers of destructive wood boring beetles would eventually run out of dead down trees and they would soon attach the remaining live standing trees. Because of their lack of knowledge in forestry, every effort was made by the environmentalist to stop the blow down removal.

Around the first of August when the tree removal was at its highest on the Copper City Sale, I got a call from the Ranger telling me I must stop all logging. The closure request was coming from the Chief of the Forest Service in Washington D.C. There had been a complaint from a very well-known person or persons that the Copper City Timber Sale was being operated outside of the agreed contract. The Chief and some of his staff would be flying in from DC the next day to investigate the illegal activity. Neither I nor my Ranger, Spike, had any idea what the illegal behavior was. I headed to the sale to stop all logging until further notice The Chief of the Forest Service would be checked things out. To all concerned this sounded REALLY BIG to have the Chief of the Forest Service come all the way from Washington DC to check out a timber sale.

The next day the Chief and his deputies arrived in Yakima at 8AM in a private plane. The Ranger and I took separate rigs to the airport in order to carry all the big-time inspectors that were with the Chief. From the airport to the Copper City Sale took over 3 hours and I don't think there were 10 words spoken in my truck. However, Spike said the Chief talked the whole time about how terrible things must have gotten to have a Supreme Court Justice come to his office and report the findings of non-compliance on the Copper City Timber Sale in Washington State and that he should get out there and straighten everyone out, and if necessary, stop all activity permanently. First off, the Sale Administrator must be removed from the sale –that was me!

When we got to the sale area we were greeted by the owners and operators of the local dude ranch, who just happen to be good friends with the Justice. They operated in the forest mostly in the upper Bumping area beyond the sale area. So now we were going to find out what the breach of contract was. The dude ranch owner claimed Webb Logging, the logging contractor for Boise Cascade, was skidding logs with a D-9 caterpillar tractor. The contract required D-6 or smaller equipment. WOW, that was a shock to me. I told the Chief and my Ranger that I had been on the sale every day since it started and the biggest tractor out in the woods skidding logs was a D-6. There were 3 D-6's and one small D-4 which could hardly pull one tree at a time. So, I took the group from DC and my Ranger to the two different landings and showed them the tractors. Since I had stopped all skidding the day before all the tractors were at the landings so they could easily see the correct size of machines. At the second landing one of the DC boys spoke out and said I must have the big tractors hid out in the trees. I was dumfounded and mad but kept my cool.

How could they think such a thing? About this time an old Euclid tractor pulling a 5-ton rock-crushing roller came up the newly rock covered road breaking oversized rocks into gravel. It was there only to pull the roller up and down the newly rocked road. This was a large tractor; yes, it was larger than a D-9 tractor; however, it had no cable drum or cables to pull logs, only a 2-foot-long hitch to hook to the rock roller. At that moment, the dude ranches owner said, "See there it is the tractor that's breaking the contract." Everyone there but the ranch owner could tell that tractor never left the road it was so large and so heavy it would have sunk up to the seat of the operator if it got 20 feet off the hard packed road and out into the very wet spongy forest. After that, the Forest Chief and my Ranger talked with the dude ranch owner for about half an hour while the rest of the group from DC and I sat without a word in our trucks. The DC personnel could not believe that they came all the way from Washington DC for something that was not happening. On the way back to the airport I was told that to satisfy the ranch owner an additional Forester would be added to the sale administration of the sale, to ensure that all contract items would be adhered to. "Or I was to be the scapegoat to all misunderstandings and be removed from Administration of that sale."

This was a bit of a blow to my pride, but I guess when politics are involved someone must take the fall to make things right in the eyes of those who think they were right. Besides the dude ranch owner had a Supreme Court Justice involved and the head of the Forest Service so they must have been right. Even though there were NO D-9's

SKIDDING LOGS on this site. I was getting behind on my Small Sales and this gave me a chance to get back to the small sale logging operators and marking, cruising, appraising, advertising, selling and administrating sales for the little guys.

The New Forester

The young man that took over the Copper City Blow Down sale was totally infatuated with Television. In the 1960's it was almost impossible to receive any sort of reception at the Ranger Station and our housing there. To fix this the Forester went to great levels to get a signal by using an old set of iron bed springs and placing them high on the hill above his forest cabin, with about 300 feet of coaxial cable back down the hill to the cabin for TV reception. Even with all this effort the best reception was late at night when all the Hwy traffic slowed down and not too many planes flying overhead. Also, at this time there were no TV recording devices so if there was something you wanted to see you had to be there at your TV to see it. What I am trying to get to is, he stayed up late most every night watching and not getting enough sleep.

About two months had passed and the Copper City Sale was closing. Landing slash had to be cleanly piled free from dirt for later burning, missed merchantable small or larger logs had to be found that might have been missed during normal skidding and removed from the forest, the short temporary roads that were built from the main road to the log landings had to be closed. We called this putting unneeded roads to bed, by roughing the surface for later planting of trees and grass, ditching for proper drainage, but most of all blocking the temp roads so no one could later use it and cause damage to the forest.

Now back to the Forester watching the sale and its contract requirements. He was staying up most every night past midnight to watch his favorite TV shows and then getting up the next morning at 5:30, in order to be on the sale area by 8AM. This was not working out too well. After several hours of driving to the sale then hiking through the logged areas looking for missed merchantable logs and marking drainage or blocking areas on temp roads, he would catch a nap in his truck. This sleeping in the truck in the afternoon had also happened during the months before this hurry-up time of the closure of the sale. Well, the inevitable happened when he was pulled into a temporary road that he had marked for closing just far enough back for no one to see him and the road was permanently closed while he was asleep. This blocked him and his truck behind a large stump and an earthen berm 4 feet high. When he awoke it was 5PM on Friday night all the loggers had gone home.

Sometime around 10PM that night, the Forester was at my door of the bunkhouse I was staying in. Someone had given him a ride down to the station after he had walked out several miles. He told me of his problem and wanted me to go back to the sale area and operate one of the tractors to free his truck.

Why he had picked me to help him was because he knew I could operate logging tractors. With my small sales work I had asked loggers for and got a few lessons to operate tractors. My purpose for learning how to operate a tractor was for safety. Not my safety but the loggers. They often worked alone and did extraordinary things, like pulling their tractor to get it started with their log truck "alone." Then after starting the tractor and both the truck and tractor are moving get out of the truck run back to put the break on the tractor then get down and run to the truck to stop its engine. After that they would get between the truck and the tractor to release the tractor. Sometimes the brakes on tractors do not work well. Now think about all the things that could go wrong with that scenario. This is one of many reasons I learned to operate a tractor, for safety reasons mine-and the operator.

I told the Forester that I would call Mr. Webb, the sale contractor, in the morning and ask permission to operate one of his machines for an hour or so. He would want to know why but I was sure he would give me the permission to use a tractor to remove the truck from the closed spur road. Sometime later that day after the call to Webb we arrived at the closed spur road and as luck would have it there was a tractor nearby-probably the one used to close that road. I reopened the road, and the forester removed his truck. Within an hour of tractor work of opening and closing the road we headed back to the Ranger Station. Funny, no words were spoken between me or the Forester at that time. Not even thanks.

Now I never told anyone except for Mr. Webb about the truck and how it got behind the closed road, but the story got out. Probably the loggers or others in the bunkhouse that night when he came for help. Anyway, within the next two months the Copper City Forester had a new job- it was in Anchorage Alaska. He had often applied to move up in rank and Alaska fulfilled that request. I was back as the Large Sale Administrator. No questions asked.   No answers given. This was not my only tussle with the local dude ranch.   Another story for another day.

I am hard at work at the Naches Ranger Station talking with logging operators. 1972.

Chapter 2

Spike and the Big Fish

On a nice sunny day only three months after I was hired, the Ranger came into my little office looking for directions to Slide Lake. I was completely taken aback; you might say blindsided. Before he came into my office, I had been total wrapped up in log scale volumes and cutting reports, the things I had been hired to do. This was totally out of the blue to be giving directions to a lake to the District Ranger. In my young and unproven self, I thought a Ranger knew where all his lakes and trails were. "Ha" guess what? I, as a Boy Scout, had covered more of his District then he had. As I later found out, the Ranger and most of his top people hardly ever get out into the forest. They manage paper and people.

Previously during my interview for my first "real" job, just out of school, Spike and his assistant asked many questions about my experience. Things like why I wanted to work for the

Forest Service. I told them of my summers of 1955, 56, and 57 were spent at Boy Scout Camp Fife as an archery instructor and day hike leader over most of the trails in the Bumping River drainage. The summer of 1958 I was working at the Philmont Boy Scout Ranch in northern New Mexico, leading senior scouts on back country 10-day trips through the Ranch. Even as a young Tender Foot through Life Scout 1951 to 1955, I had accompanied my troop on weekend hikes in the Little Naches and Milk Creek area on trails leading to lakes and such. All of this gave me the knowledge and wish to work in the forest when I was older.

Now I realized that Spike had tuned in on my experience and wanted and needed more info on some lakes he had heard about. As it turned out in the early 1950s the Game Department planted fish in many small lakes that were hard to get to and off the beaten path. This was to encourage hikers and fishermen to go deeper into the forest for adventures (also to sell more fishing licenses). Well as it turned out Spike had tried to find the lake the past weekend with no luck even with using aerial photos.

To speed things up and find this Devils Slide Lake, Spike said that "the next day I was to lead him into the lake." It would be a discovery day to learn more about his District, fishing poles and all.   Things were quite a bit different from the time I had hiked the Milk Creek trail as a 12-year-old. We had hiked from Hwy 410 up the trail; my best guess was about 4 ½ miles. But now in1959 there was a new Forest Logging road somewhat running parallel the old trail. So, I checked the map of the area and remembered that at about 4 miles up the trail we came across a section line crossing, a metal sign telling which section you were in, and blazes on the trees. At that point we followed the blazes of the section line to the lake.

Well as you may surmise my Ranger was quite impressed as I drove up the road to the section line crossing and told him to get his things together as we need to hike in from this point. It was a short hike, maybe a half mile, to the lake.

We spent more than an hour trying every kind of bait: flies, worms, and maggots, both with and without bobbers. When we started our leader, the line was heavy (thick), so we changed to thin line but no luck. Nothing worked. That lake had all sorts of natural food in it, basically all the fish had to do was open its mouth and food flowed in.

Now these fish had been in this lake for over 15 years, starting out as one to two-inch fingerlings. Well, I am sure they had reproduced some of their own offspring by now as we could see small 2- inch fish near the shore and bigger fish surfacing further out. We had no idea as to how large they may be.

Spike put on his thinking hat (joke) and looked around for something to use as bait. Something more natural for the fish, something to get their attention. And as I was looking also, I saw Spike tearing apart a rotten log. I thought he must be looking for grubs (small worm-like larva), but now suddenly, he jumped over the log and grabbed a baby shrew (a type of mouse). That was a first for me.

Believe what you want but that was going to be his bait. He hooked his fishing hook into the shrew through the skin on its back, so it had full range of motion. Then he placed the little mouse on a 6-8-inch-wide piece of bark. The mouse and the bark were set adrift on the lake. Once the bark had drifted some 30+ feet out on the lake the shrew was jerked off the bark into the water. The mouse began to swim back towards the bark, but out of the deep came what we knew was the biggest freshwater fish either of us had ever seen.

Now the game was on and the Ranger had to keep his cool for he still had the light leader line on his pole. It was quite a sight: Spikes line fed out with a screaming sound and the fish went to the center and bottom of the lake. When the line stopped going out Spike started reeling it in as smooth and steady as he could without tugging too hard due to the light fish line. He would almost get the big fish to the shore and then back out to the center of the lake it would go. That in and out went on two more times until the big lonker tired out and had no more fight. I would say it took over 12 maybe 15 minutes before Spike got the fish to the shore.

Now for all you so-called fisherman, Spike netted the 23-inch 2+ lb. Eastern Brook Trout, weighed and measured it then put it back into the water and watched it swim away. His reason not to keep the fish was, "if we needed food to eat, I would keep it, but we don't" So now we have fish to come back to.

Chapter 3

Little Boy Lost -September 1961

Day One: Sometime in the early morning, prior to normal work hours, Spike, our District Ranger at the time, came banging on the bunk house door. I let him in to find he had an assignment for me that did not meet my normal timber job duties. He told me that I was to be the go-between for the Forest Service, Sherriff, Army, and Citizen Volunteers on a Search and Rescue for a 12-year-old boy lost in the Twin Sister Lake area of the Cougar Lakes Limited area. (Upper Bumping Lake area) And, as always in my new career with the Forest Service, it was "get your pants and boots on and get there **Yesterday**." I was 21 years old and in my third year with the Forest Service.

I loaded up my Forest Service truck with water, quick meals ready-to-eat military canned food, and that ever-so-lightweight Forest Service radio, 26 lbs.+ extra batteries, and my sleeping bag.

About the portable radio: it was the latest thing for the Forest Service. Before these new radios became available the only radios we had were mounted in the trucks and at base stations. You could pack the portable with you anywhere in the forest and have some confidence that maybe someone would hear you. But with all our other Forest Service gear: unless you had a horse or a short hike, you probably left the radio in the truck to save time and your back.

It was about normal work time, and I was off to the Bumping Lake road and trail head at Deep Creek Campground. Spike told me that Buss and Pappy, they were our Back-Country Horsemen, would be coming in later that day on horseback to the Twin Sister Lake area. They would be coming in with pack horses bringing camping gear, and a tent and table for map layout, to the Lake area. One of them would then help me set up a Base Camp for the searchers to get information and coordinate the search in the Wilderness. The other man on horseback would start looking for the boy.

The trail ahead of me to Little Twin Lake was about a 2 ½ mile hike. The local News Media had just arrived about this time at the end of the Deep Creek road and were setting up shop, getting info for the Evening News about the lost boy. So before heading up to Little Twin Lake I told them what I knew about the lost boy.

On the day before 3 boys of 10 to 12 years old, one named Harry and a middle-age man, an Uncle I think, were hiking up to Big Twin Lake carrying a lightweight aluminum boat. Two at a time would carry the boat, they would rest and the other two would carry. As the story goes, they were almost to the first lake, Little Twin when the man and young Harry had just finished with their turn to carry. Harry was excited and wanted to run on ahead to see the lake, so they agreed to let him go on ahead but not to leave the trail. Some twenty to thirty minutes later the two remaining boys and the man reached the Little Sister Lake with the boat. But Harry was not there. They called, they waited, and then they searched. But young Harry was not to be found. While they were searching, they came across a young couple who helped them look for Harry. After an afternoon of searching, it was almost dark. The young couple said they would stay at the first lake overnight and watch for Harry, this would allow the uncle and the two boys to go down and gather more people to help search. There are many lakes, 60+ in this area, so their staying would make a good starting point the next day. That is where we are now, setting up a search.

As I was starting up the trail the Sheriff volunteer Back Country Horsemen arrived and offered me a horse to ride up to the lake. I told the leader of the group 'no thanks' that they needed their horses and that I was in fair shape for the 2 ½ mile hike. I could see that the horses and the volunteers were out-of-shape. They would only slow me down. I arrived one hour ahead of the Horsemen at Little Twin. It was a steep trail, and I am sure they made many stops for the horses to rest.

By the close of the first day the Base Tent was set up, maps out, and two Army Reserve 5-Man squads were searching the near areas of up to ½ mile all around Little Twin Lake. The Sherriff Horseman had traveled all over the Mosquito Valley from Tumac Mountain to Fryingpan Lake and back to Little Twin.   But no Little Harry to be found.

There are many trails once you reach the Mosquito Valley area which includes the Twin Sisters Lakes. There are human trails and animal trails that crisscross the 15+ sq. mile basin. All these trails are confusing to even the best of high-country hikers.

It was a restless night. People and family calling and hiking all around the valley with flashlights. The other misguiding thing about Mosquito Valley besides the trails are the lakes they are everywhere. <u>With a quick look at the Forest Service map on the last page of this story, you can see over 60 small lakes in this area.</u> Oh, and by the way, there are millions of mosquitoes per sq. foot in the summer mostly after dark. When hiking or camping after dark you do not need extra protein for energy just take a breath with your mouth open.

Day Two. More volunteers, horsemen, all the Forest Service personnel the district could spare due to fire season, and the Army Reserve men were at Base Camp just after daylight. On this day I had drawn up special maps for the horseman to travel even further west to Jug Lake and then south east towards Dumbbell Lake. The horsemen's instructions were to zig zag back and forth around as many of the small lakes as they had time. As it worked out, they split up into two groups so they could cover more ground. The Forest Service personnel were sent north towards Fish Lake after they made a sweep of Big Twin Sister Lake. Volunteers were sent south to Henry Lake, and then west to Snow Lake and any little lake in-between. The Army reserve men had the duty of spreading out in a swath about 50 feet apart and move through all the immediate lakes within ½ mile of Big and Little Twin Lakes. By the end of the day 75 men and women and 14 horses and riders had covered most of Mosquito Valley with a fine-tooth comb. So many searchers, so many lakes but no little Harry was to be found.

Day Three. Spirits were low but new volunteers and most of the original volunteers, horsemen, and Army and Forest Service personnel, were there at daylight and ready for new assignments. I sent everyone back to yesterday's assignment, but this time I told them to investigate the water of each lake or pond. My fear was he may have tried to swim in the heat the day he arrived and drowned or traveling at night fell into one.

About 10 AM, George, a horseman from Tieton, and his neighbor Ike came riding into Base Camp wanting to help.   I told George and Ike that I doubted young Harry was alive, with all the people and the country covered the last 3 days he should have shown up. So, my best guess was he probably took a swim in the heat of the day, after his hard hike up to the lakes and drowned. And since you cowboys know how to get around on horseback, would you ride your horses as far out into and around Big Twin Lake as possible to look for a body. They agreed and left with one more special tool to find a boy: **a dog**.

Well sometime around noon Ike came riding back into Base Camp as fast and as safe as he could on his big gelding horse. He had a smile as wide as a country mile. He was yelling as he came thundering into Camp, that they had found the boy and he was alive. He wanted me to take his horse and ride over to the back side of Big Twin, which would be the north side. I asked Ike if the boy needed first aid and Ike said all he needs is food, love, and a bath to help clean up all the mud and blood from mosquito bites. I made a quick call on the Forest Service radio to let everyone know that little Harry had been found alive. I also said before I signed off that they should stay tuned after I have seen the boy, I would let everyone know 'What's What and Why' about his condition.

With that Ike and I rode double over to the where George was holding the boy up next to him in order to warm him. The boy was holding the dog tight to him. For the next hour or so we gave Harry water and small amounts of food, so not to make him sick due to the lack of real food for 3+ days. He was found with his pockets full of tall grass and berry stains on his face. George was trying to have a conversation with Harry when we got to where they were. But the only words I heard from young Harry for that hour was "more food and nice doggy."

Back at Base Camp the Army EMT's checked Harry over and cleaned him up, gave him some dry clean clothes, even though they were two sizes too big and Army issue at that. About that time the Sherriff Volunteers showed up and offered to give Harry a horseback ride down the trail to Deep Creek Campground and to his waiting family. Harry looked at George and Ike and said a few more words, finally: "can they take me on their horses with their dog too?"   But before George and Ike left with Harry, George came over to me and said quietly "You did not have to hide that boy for 3 days in order to let me find him. I already like you as a friend of my daughter." We had a good laugh. Now there is another story: George was a farmer and a good horseman from Tieton Washington and the father of a young waitress I was dating from Whistling Jacks Restaurant which was just 2 miles from the Naches Ranger Station I call that coincidental.   But thank God George and Ike showed up with that dog.

By now the Forest Service horse packers were there to clean up the Base Camp and remove all the gear, tables, tent, food, water, and garbage, etc. And it was my time to head out, I jogged down the trail by myself, thinking over all that had transpired the last 3 days. Almost as quick as I started, and in a blink of an eye, I was next to my waiting truck at the Campground. Deep Creek Campground was full of News people, family of Harry, volunteers, Sherriff Posse, and well-wishers, but I had enough excitement and just got in my truck and headed back to the Ranger Station to home and a much-needed shower.

Now there are many questions as to how Harry could not have been found sooner, with volunteers, Army and Forest Service personnel, all around both Twin Lakes every day and even that morning before George and Ike found him. I believe Harry survived by eating berries and tall grass and drinking water from small streams. Somehow by himself that first afternoon and evening, because no one went close to Big Twin, where he was waiting, he became frightened and fearful of all humans and he reverted to an animal state of mind to be weary of people and their sounds. What made the difference in the search and in locating Harry was the DOG_ George said that while they were searching and calling for him, Harry came out of the brush and grabbed on to the dog and would not let go.

Now What Boy Does Not Love A Dog?

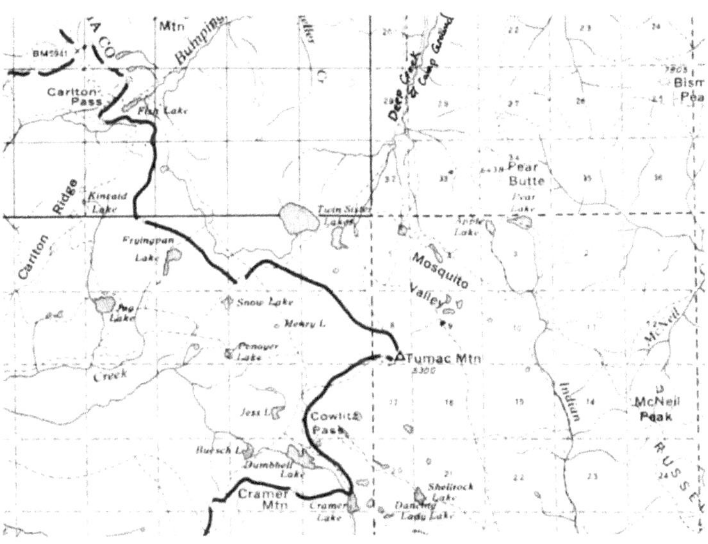

The map of lakes

Chapter 4

Horseshoe Bend with Einsom-My First Dog

I was driving to Yakima with my Weimaraner, Einsom, in my 56 Ford; it was late in November after a light snowfall. I was driving at about 45 MPH on slushy snow, but when I went into the shade of the canyon leading to Horseshoe Bend the Slush went to ice. As I took my foot off the gas the car started to skid towards the river. I pumped the breaks, but the Ford seemed to speed up. I thought through all possibilities of what to do to stop the direction and speed of the car. Nothing worked, I was about to just jump out when the car hit the edge of the road and turned sideways with drivers' side down. (this was before seat belts) The door popped open and the next thing I knew I was out of the car on my back and it was coming at me. I quickly put one foot on the driver's seat and the other on the door jamb (the door was already torn off). The sliding sideways Ford pushed me towards the river, skipping over large boulders, tearing my denim jacket as we went. I kept my head up to keep it from hitting one of those large rocks, while I skipped along ahead of the car. Just a few feet from the river's edge the car bounced up and turned front end towards the water and I somehow was under the car when it stopped. My left ankle was pinned by the car frame and a large flat rock (I had western boots on that's what probably saved my ankle from being totally crushed). I tried to free myself by pulling up on the mufflers but was unable to free myself; all I got was a burnt wrist from the hot muffler. My head and legs were out of the water, but my back was in a pool and if I tilted my head back it was under water.

From under the car, I could see Horseshoe Bend and cars coming West towards where I left the road, however they did not stop or see me or my car down in the river. About this time my dog that was still in the car got out whining as though he had been hurt in the crash to the river. He tried to come to me but there was no room to crawl in. He kept whining I told him to go get help. He turned and headed up to the road where he sat and waited. A few minutes later a friend and neighbor, Mrs. R, driving home, spotted my dog sitting on the edge of the road where we had slid off. She stopped to see why he was there, and I shouted as loud as I could and got her attention as to where I was. Mrs. R, bewildered as she was shouting to me, asking if I was OK and as far as I knew I was fine, but needed help getting the car off me. She flagged down other folks who then tried to lift the car off, but 3 young men could not. I told one of the men who stopped to help that they needed a lever (a long stout pole) to pry the car up. I told him how to enter my trunk and get an ax to chop down a pole for leverage. He did and they levered the car off my ankle. Einsom was there as I slid out from under the car to lick my face. I thanked all the people that had stopped to help and reassured my neighbor that I was OK and that she should go on home.

By then the Naches Wrecker was there to pull my car up from the river. The car was aprox.90 to 100 feet down the road embankment into the edge of the river. There was not much to do other than hook up to the axle and pull the car up to the road. The Wrecker driver, the State Patrolman, and I all knew the car would be totally wrecked by the time it was dragged up to the road. Well, the front bumper, the front grill, the oil pan and the door would need to be repaired or replaced but that was all. And my luck was still coming in. Two of George Layman's mill people were out of work for a while, due to a fire at the mill. As it was, they were top body and fender guys that worked on Race cars. So, my repair was not going to cost me and arm and leg. As it turned out just Parts and labor, thank God for the honesty of the local repair shop in Naches and that he had hired those out of work mill men during the time the Layman's Lumber Mill was rebuilt...Oh and I got a $25 ticket for driving too fast and leaving the road. It was 1961, today that would have cost me $2,500 and I did know the Patrolman, I think that helped.

Einsom's last act was as a hero to a near-by family when he saved 2 children's lives from a speeding car. A distracted driver failed to see Einsom and two small children near the side of the road, striking Einsom. His body blocked the blow, protecting the children from injury but causing his death.

He is my first canine hero!

Chapter 5

My Pals Stag and Snooper

You have not heard of my second dog, Stag, or my saddle horse, Snooper, so I will bring you up to date on them. In 1962 I purchased 2 riding horses-one was a tall strong sorrel mare, the second was a stout Pinto. The pinto was a sharp looking animal under saddle, but shortly after I purchased him, he had a Botfly Larva come out through his back. The area of its exit was dead center under where the saddle would sit and as it turned out more time was spent doctoring the sore area then riding the horse. Because of my short patience and a full year of trying to mend this scabbed area, I sold the pinto to a young woman who only wanted it for it looks in her small pasture and not to ride. With its sale I had sufficient capital to hunt for a match to my big Sorrel mare, an equally tall and dark red saddle horse. As I was searching, I put out the word to some of the Forest Service crew friends. Well, with no big fanfare Ed G. found the right horse for me. Ed was an assistant log scaler for the F.S. He talked to his cousin who worked at the Yakima Racetrack who knew of a young Quarter Horse that had a minor leg crack. The leg had healed but he could not race again. This was my once in a lifetime opportunity to own a young 3-year-old quarter horse, with the color and the size I wanted. He was named Snooper on the Quarter Horse registry, and that name fit him quite well for how he would act over the years.

Of course, Snooper and I had a few go-rounds because of his racehorse training and my more laid-back approach to mounting and starting off to ride slow and easy. He was ready to run as soon as you put a foot in the stirrups.

Goat Rock Wilderness—Stag and Taylor's Horse Sam keeping watch while Ken and I rest. ©K Taylor

In order to keep him from running out from under me as I mounted, I would have to point him at a tree, a barn, a fence or anything he could not go over. This mounting exercise lasted our whole partnership. He never got over wanting to start fast.

My first horse 'Lady' with wife, Bonnie, on the left and me on Snooper on the right, near Cougar Lake on the Naches Ranger District. ©K Taylor

Snooper was young and ambitious when I purchased him. He had been hand-treated almost from the day he was born because of his promise to be a great Quarter Horse racehorse. Well now at the age of 3 he was put in a 2-acre pasture with one other horse, Lady, and nothing to do but eat and wait for me and a weekend of trail riding.

The pasture was fenced off near a young family's trailer house home which had children and the young couple coming and going all the time. With all these people around, but no one paying Snooper the time of day, he was bored and wanted attention. He would often stand day after a day in the corner of the fence near the trailer trying to attract attention. Occasionally someone would give him a clump of grass or just rub his soft nose- however this was not enough attention for him. One day when the young mother was hanging her laundry out to dry, she noticed that Snooper had his foot hanging through the fence. The foot was kind of propped over the lowest barbed wire strand just 12 inches off the ground. Thinking he needed help she immediately ran over to him and lifted the foot off the wire. She told me later that she checked for cuts but there were none. After petting and talking to him for a few minutes she left to finish her laundry. About an hour or so later she told me that when she came out to drive to the store, he was fine. Fine as in the manner of speaking. Before she could get the car out of the driveway Snooper had his foot in the fence again, she removed it and left for the store. Returning from the store she saw he was out feeding in the pasture doing fine, but while she was unloading the groceries he was back at the fence with his foot through the fence. That evening she told me of his actions and her concerns that he may hurt himself and that I should replace the barbed wire and put in pole railing. I got a big laugh and apologized for laughing. I told her to ignore him and he will stop being a pill over time when no one comes to his rescue.

Stag and Snooper often played rough with each other. There were times Stag would bring an empty burlap feed sack and drag it in front of Snooper as if teasing him. Snooper would grab the sack in his teeth and give Stag a fling out across the pasture which would bring Stag back with the bag to see if Snooper could get it from him with a playful taunt.

Taylor (an old friend) and I were going for a horseback ride one Saturday morning, both our horses and Stag loaded in the back of my truck. Stag, when in the horse truck rode in the feed rack up front where the horse's heads were tied. We were headed up the 410 Hwy at about 45 miles an hour, when we felt the truck sway and heard a loud bang like a horse kicking the side boards. Then BANG! In the middle of my trucks' motor hood was Stag spread out on all fours trying to hang onto the flat smooth hood and not fall off onto the Hwy. Taylor immediately opened his door and stepped out on the running board and grabbed onto Stag to keep him from sliding off onto the road. I slowed the truck to a stop to keep all safe -Taylor and dog. As soon as Taylor lowered Stag to the ground he headed to the back of the truck and wanted to get back up there with Snooper. I am sure more trouble would come so until they had cooled off from whatever started their feud, he would ride up front with us in the cab. After a long horseback ride up American Ridge that afternoon, the ride home was quiet. No Horse Play. Evidently earlier Snooper got his nose under Stag up there in the feed loft and flipped him out on to the hood. That would have been a good one for a picture.

Often, I did not have a lot of time to hunt deer when the Logging was going hot and heavy, so I would from time-to-time saddle Snooper as soon as I got home from work and we would ford the river behind our house at Rock Creek on Hwy 410. I could get in an hour or two before the sun would go down and then quickly cross back to our place as the day ended. Once across the river I would dismount Snoop and put the reins up so he could move freely behind me and grab a bite of grass if he wanted. Snooper would follow along behind me step for step. If I moved fast, he did the same, if I slowed, he crept along behind as quiet as a 1,000-pound horse could. If I stopped to check out a draw or far-off hill he would stop and often look over my shoulder in the same direction. It was like I had a second set of eyes. In all the times we did this sort of hunt we never saw a legal buck but lots of does. Oh, another Snooper quirk: if I ever brought the gun up to my shoulder to check out a deer through the scope, Snooper would back away from me at least 20 feet or more. I am sure he did not like the noise if I were to shoot. Other than that, he was always right with me step for step.

Most years after hay season was over, I pastured my horses at Sprick's down the road. Sprick had three large hay fields and the field at the North end of his property was where I corralled my horses till the snow came in October or November. The fields were across the road from the Bald Mountain road, about a mile south of our home at Rock Creek. Well, it was getting late in the year, maybe almost December, there was no snow cover in the Pasture, so I left the horses longer than normal at Spricks.' I do not know whose idea it was but one morning early I heard Stag outside the back-door barking and the sound of horse hoofs in the gravel driveway. I got up to find Snooper, Lady, and her last year's colt in the driveway looking at my hay shed, which was blocked by my truck, so they could not get to the hay. As I found out later from neighbors and one of Webb's Logging truck drivers that the 4 of them came up Highway 410 from Sprick's Pasture single file on the shoulder of the road facing traffic just like

Stag always did when he went visiting. I guess they thought I forgot to come and bring them home for winter, so they did it themselves. I think it was all Stags idea to bring his buddy and friends home for winter. All I had to do was open the corral gate and all three horses went into the corral and stood waiting for hay as if they had done a good job and wanted praise and payment for it! The hay field at Spricks' and lower field were all well fenced with barbed wire on post that went well into the river to where it was over 4 feet deep in summer, however it was not summer now and the water was low, so they just walked around the ending post in the river and came home, up the highway.

On most overnight horse trips, it was customary to hobble the horses at night to let them feed on mountain meadows. Usually, we would un-hobble and bring them in close to camp before dark so they would not wander off and get lost. However, in this particular camp at Cement Basin it was a perfect bowl and the only way out was through camp. It had been a long day of riding and the horses needed more feed, so we left them hobbled to feed all night. To our surprise both Snooper and Lady were smack dab in the middle of camp come daylight. I had to crawl out the back of the tent to get out. They were standing between the tent and the fire-pit leaving no room to move past them. I am sure they were more interested in getting their oats for the day then fresh coffee. On this same trip Snooper played a trick on me while I was trying to saddle up Lady. I put her saddle blanket on then turned and picked up the pack saddle, while I was turned Snooper took the saddle blanket off Lady so when I tried to saddle her-no blanket! I put down the saddle and replaced the blanket. Again, I reached down for the saddle and Snooper removed the blanket. I saw him this time -JOKE OVER- I moved him away and finished the job.

This one I wished I had taken pictures of. It was a long snowy winter and the corral next to our driveway where I kept the horses in winter to be close and easy to feed was in deep snow. This winter it was very deep in snow. Over time with each snowfall the horses packed down the snow next to the fence to almost 4 ½ feet high. All you could see was the top rail of a 3-rail fence. From the house or anywhere you could see the corral it looked like the horses were held in by an 18-inch-high fence. They never tried to step over the low fence. It is a good thing because it would have been a long way down on the outside of the corral, as there was no packed snow there.

Stag and I were checking on the cleanup of a small Timber Sale on what is called Devils Creek Rim. There had been several trees that had blown down that winter and a quick sale was made to remove the trees to avoid the loss of the lumber and the possible build up in numbers of Pine Beatles. Pine Beatles attack dead or down trees, and if they are not removed quickly their numbers grow and then they attack live standing trees. As I was checking the tree removal, I saw a Mountain Goat eating the moss from the blow-down trees. This was quite unusual since the Mountain Goats are normally at a much higher elevation and miles away on American and Fife's Ridge area. I contacted the local Game Warden thinking it may be a sick or old Goat run off from the herd. Shortly after, the Warden arrived as we were approaching the area where I saw the Goat, I heard Stag squeal and yelp as in fear. Then out of the trees came a young Calf Elk and not too far behind it was Stag running at full speed. MAN, this did not look good- my dog chasing a calf elk in front of the Game Warden. But wait, a second later the mother Elk appeared and was right on Stags tail (so to speak). Stag took a hard right and the calf went straight but the mother Elk was not letting him off so easily. She continued pursuit and chased Stag for another hundred yards and then circled back to her calf. The Game Warden and I figured Stag was not chasing the Calf but running from the mother after he came too close to her calf and she went after him. Stag spent the rest of the day at my side. He did not get more than two feet away. That was a lesson learned for Stag: do not get close to wild animal babies.

On my way to the Nile area and another Timber Sale to check out, I came upon a rare sight. From my right side just fifty feet ahead of the truck a Mother Skunk and her litter of six, at least, darted in front of my FS truck, I slammed on the breaks and came to a stop just a few feet from them. Now Stag was standing right behind the truck cab with his feet up on the rail so he could look around the cab forward (his normal position). He saw them. My thoughts were "oh no" he may jump down onto them, but NO he slowly backed down into the truck bed out of sight of the Skunks. He was better prepared then I. My driver's side window was down, and I got a rather good whiff before I got it up and she and her clan made it across the road and out of sight. In all the years Stag traveled with me and his alone travels, he never came home smelling like a skunk or with porky pine quills stuck in him. It was like he had a 7th sense to never go close to other animals that may hurt you.

The only time I ever saw Stag fight happened one early morning when I was on my way to a Timber Sale in the Little Naches Drainage. I had received a radio call to go the Pine Cone Inn and inform them they had an emergency and needed to come down to the Ranger Station to make a phone call to inquire about the emergency. This was 1966 or 67 and, in those days, there were no phones above the Naches Ranger Station, so if you made a call there was a pay phone at the Pond Cafe located just a mile below the Ranger Station. In an emergency people called the Naches Ranger Station to request the Ranger to help locate the person in need. Well, Stag was in the back of my Forest Service truck as he liked to ride and when I parked at the Pine Cone Inn, I told Stag to stay in the truck while I delivered the news. Just after I delivered the bad news, I heard a loud commotion and barking outside. I ran out to find the Pine Cones' children's Black Lab in the back of my Forest Service truck with Stag. I was completely shocked. How did this Lab get in the truck? Stag had this big Lab by the throat in a death grip. I jumped into the bed of the truck not knowing what to do- Stag had no collar to grab in order to pull him away from the Lab, so I kicked Stag in the side. Before I could pull my foot back from the kick, Stag had turned and bit me on the toe of my boot. His death-fight-grip went through the top of my boot into the flesh of my foot. When Stag heard my voice and saw what he had done to me he immediately let go of his bite. As soon as the Lab was free from Stags grip, he jumped out of the truck and ran into the Inn. The Pine

Cone boys told me years later that their big strong Lab never picked a fight again. Lucky for me I had received a tetanus shot just the month before due to a cut I got from shoeing my horse. P.S. I did check the Lab out before I left to be sure he would not bleed to death. The folks at Pine Cone Inn said their dog picked the fight so no blame on Stag for protecting the truck.

Oh, and about my kids. Do not move too quickly towards one of them if Stag is nearby you may lose a bit of your pants or blood or both. Just ask Mrs. Bill W, he kept them safe from even getting to close to the bluff behind them in this picture. Stag shadowed them if they left our yard.

Duane & Kim & Stag ©Dale X Phipps

Chapter 6

Naches Ranger District Parties

The Naches Ranger District, when I started work there, had a tradition of family and adult parties. Parties for retirement, welcome parties for new Foresters or Engineers, there were going away parties for those moving to new areas, and the Christmas and New Year's parties. We were a very close-knit group of 9 or 10 families who helped one another and watched after each other, work or play. Being 30 miles from Yakima, poor phone service, no TV, and long winters we got to know each other quite well.

The party thing all started for me and Norma one fall day in 1962. (Norma was my assistant with log scale accounts and cutting reports). She did things I could never have done while I worked in the field as I did on timber sales. She was my total backup and believe me kept me out of a lot of trouble.

Back to the start of our part in the Ranger Station parties. Spike, our Ranger, came up stairs to our office that Fall day with a big smile and a request. His request started like this," I would like you and Norma to put together a family-type dinner party for a departing Forester and his family heading to a new forest." Now the request coming from your boss was quite a jolt. Neither Norma nor I had completed anything like that before, so I am sure Spike could see our confusion. There was a place needed for the dinner, a caterer needed for food, gifts purchased for an up-and-coming Forester, notices for the upcoming party. Also, mailings of the notice to those families that did not live on the compound, and the matter of how we would pay for all this. Spike kind of put us at ease by saying there was a money machine in the Ready Room to help with payments of rent and gifts and dinner for the guest of honor and his family, everyone else would pay for their own meal.

The "Ready Room" was a large open area in the carpenter's shop where all field-going personnel met each morning to get their jobs assignments and crews together. In the summer season there were as many as 30 personnel due to temporary workers. The "Money Machine" was a Coke-Cola machine. Of course, Norma and I found out we also had a new job: ordering pop, keeping the machine full, and collecting the money from the machine. Now we were not getting rich. The cost per bottle from the pop machine was 25 cents and the Stations profit was 5 cents a bottle. With so many young people coming and going there always seemed to be $100.00+ to work with on the gifts and accommodations for parties.

I guess we did too good of a job, because for the next 10+ years our second job was tending the pop machine and organizing parties. We were quite lucky on Christmas and New Year's parties as we rented the local Library and Nile Club House. We also invited the whole Nile Valley and Chinook Pass residents to join us, which made our extended family even stronger. Better neighbors and more people to look out for each other in an area far from police, fire protection, poor phone connections, power outages up to 6-7 days in winter due to snow.

Well sometime around 1965, 66, 67 things really got to hopping there were lots of new people coming and going. The many new personnel plus Rangers and Assistant Rangers put a stress on our pop machine payout. And on top of that keeping track of bottles was a pain. We had to threaten the crew to bring the bottles back or we would shut down the service. After that we talked it over with the Coke delivery person and he exchanged the bottle machine for a can machine, still 25 cents per can. Life was on our side when I saw advertisements from local stores selling 12 packs of Coke and its other flavors at ridiculously low prices around holidays to bring in customers. As it turned out the cost to us was about 15 cents a can, making our profit 10 cents a can per purchase. I drove to those stores in Yakima and filled up my 1956 Ford with I think 20 maybe 30, 12-packs of Coke product. The front end of my car was pretty light on the road. Well with doubling our returns on our money machine we were able to cover all the new promotion and retirements of the mid-1960's. I guess we were not buying enough products from the Coke distributor and around 1979 they removed our money machine. It really did not matter by 1980 the Ranger District office was moved to the town of Naches and the crews could buy their pop at the local stores.

With the advent of the two Ranger Stations merging and moving down the passes from White and Chinook to the town of Naches, most all the closeness of different sections of the Districts was lost. It is "come to work at 8 and go home at 5" and maybe have a beer at the local pub with your section i.e., Timber, Fire, Recreation, Wildlife-if someone is moving on.

I know this story is kind of simple, but it just goes to show that with a little thought and kindness, those folks from the 60's are all still friends even though they are spread all over the United States. It has been over 50 years and from time to time we get together by E-mail, phone calls, cards and letters and when we can, attend graduations of each other's children or now grandchildren, and old friend's funerals. There is even a retiree's picnic each fall somewhere in the area of the old Ranger District for those who can attend. As you may gather, I still have great feelings for the Old Days and the simple dumb things we did for each other. It was a time people talked and played with their fellow workers, even reached out to each other without being asked to do so.

Chapter 7

Snow Survey Morse Creek 1962

In the 1950's and 60's Snow Surveys were made by the U.S. Forest Service for the Yakima Valley Irrigation managers. The Surveys were made to acquire information of how much water was in the snow pack each year before the spring snow melt. From this information the area dams were controlled as to how much water could be released for agriculture, and not so much as to affect the health of the fish in the rivers below them. Surveys were made once a month in January, February, and March. These surveys were made by hand in the Morse Creek drainage about 3 miles in from HWY 410, to an area which is known as Morse Lake. (Today the surveys are made by electronic weight and measures which are operated by solar power.)

Larry and I prepared for our long day of cold weather

snow shoeing, and snow depth measuring at 5:30 AM before leaving the Naches Ranger Station. We put together two packs to carry safety equipment and the tubes to measure and weigh the snow. The tubes we used for measuring snow are hollow aluminum and 4 inches in diameter and 4 feet in length, which attach to each other for up to 20 feet long.

We reached the junction of HWY 410 and the Morse Creek in our F.S. truck at about 6:45 AM. After putting on our packs and snowshoes and headed up the Morse Creek road. We found the road was covered with approx. 6 feet of snow. With all the gear and the deep powdery snow, it was slow going it was now about 10:30 and we were looking at an open hillside (covered in snow but no trees) and we thought if we cut across that hill side, we could shorten our hike to the Survey area. So, we took turns leading the way up across the slope, probably a 1,000 ft. climb up from the creek bottom that we started from. It was hard going we were sinking into the snow about to our knees even though we had Sherpa snowshoes on. BY 12:15 we were at the top and into the trees for another ¼ mile of snowshoeing to the survey area. 12:45PM

Time was not on our side as we wanted to be done with the survey and back to the truck before dark (15:30). So, we took out our measuring tubes and began our survey. We started pushing the tubes down into the snow and we were adding the fourth tube when we finally reached the bottom at 13 and ½ feet of snow with a water content of 57 inches. Sometime after the second or third measurement we heard a rumbling off in the distance, we did not think too much of it (maybe snow falling out of trees? After measuring 10 different spots at 30 feet apart it was almost 14:00. Time to pack up and head out, so back tracking to the open slope we climbed in the morning would be the quickest way out. When we got to the open hill side all the snow that was on that slope had rolled to the bottom of the hill in large round balls of upwards of 20 feet in diameter.

What had happened was that after we crossed the slope creating an angled cut in the upper surface of the snowy hillside and the warmth of the mid-day and avalanche was created? Thank God it did not happen when we were crossing the slope, we would have been covered up with hundreds of feet of snow at the bottom of the creek.

We took off our snow shoes and climbed down to the creek bottom since there was no snow on the slope. The avalanched snow at the bottom was hard packed so we could climb over it as though it were large boulders. Once across the slide area (16:45 time again was not on our side), snow shoes were put back on and down the road to the waiting truck. We did not get out before dark, but with the brightness of the snow and our tracks from the morning hike in, we did just fine. It was well after 1900 when we reached the Naches Ranger Station.

Larry worked at the Naches RD for three more years before moving on to another Ranger District. But each spring the memory of that day came rushing back, and every crew that went out for that survey we warned them of the open slope and Not to Cross It. Two FOOLS were enough

This next picture shows the use of a core tube to

measure the depth of the snow at Morse Creek

Some winters that core tube had to be 16 feet long to measure the total snow depth. © picture courtesy of K. Taylor

Chapter 8

Motorcycle Gang

It all started sometime in early July when we (the Forest Service) were notified by the Yakima County Sherriff Office that we should be on the lookout for a Bicycle Gang that was on HWY 410 out of Tacoma, WA. and its destination was not known.

Now in the 1960s down south in California, Nevada, Arizona, and New Mexico each Summer large groups of the Hells Angels gang, would cruise around what seemed like looking for trouble. There were so many at a time that Police and Sherriff personnel would follow them at a distance but not provoke them. (They would stop 50 or more of them at a gas station a shopping center, or grocery store and all the people there would leave in fear.)   The reason the police followed was to make the public feel safe. But from what I heard from the local Sherriff who worked our area of the Forest, they were more scared than the public that they may have to get involved and try to arrest one or more for misdeeds.

It was sometime around 1 AM on this July night, (I know the time for I had just climbed into bed, I had been up to Whistling Jacks until 12:30PM trying to make points with one of their waitresses. I heard loud footsteps and a bang on the Bunkhouse door.

Not knowing who it maybe I put on my pants; it could be the Fire Control Officer looking for help on a possible fire left by campers? But no, it was (big) Bill our new Assistant Ranger (and he was carrying a baseball bat) Now when I say Big Bill, he was 6 feet 6 inches + at least a full head taller they myself, and what the loggers call a large man (Two ax-handles across the shoulders and about 260 LBS). Bill had previously been in the Navy for 20 years in Submarines and Air Craft Carriers, before going back to school and Forestry-he had seen a thing or two in this wild world-hence the baseball bat instead of a firearm.

Bill had been awakened by campers from Cottonwood Camp and they were frightened from their camp site by a Biker Gang. The campers had packed up their tent and belongings and left the camp in fear for their life and come to the Ranger Station to report the Gang. Now Bill's instructions to me were put on your uniform and strap on your 38. He explained the earlier evening visit he had to me and that we should go and see if other campers needed assistance.

We took separate Forest Service Trucks to make our approach look larger than two people in one truck. As we entered the camp only one area was lit by a camp fire, we could see Motorbikes by three other sites. Bills truck headed straight to the camp with a fire and the only people moving about.

Big Bill stepped out bat in hand, and I was only 4 or 5 steps behind him. He walked up to the only Biker up moving about at about 2AM. Things did not look that bad, but Bill was cautious and spoke to the biker with authority, with questions of how many were they and how long did they plan to stay. Before the Biker could answer, Bill stuck out his hand for the Biker to shake and said "Well, I'll be a Sun of a Gun, you're from the Princeton (air craft carrier) I served on it also. What Bill had seen in that flash of camp fire light was an insignia on the biker's jacket of the USS Princeton Air Craft Carrier. Well as you might size up, things went smoothly thereafter. Bill and his fellow sailor were off to tales of Navy and Korean War. As he talked about their stay and when they planned to leave the camp, I took a stroll around the other camp sites to see if other campers were there and needed consoling. But no one was in the camp but the Bikers (who knew others may have left before we got there.)

What we had come to find out the Bikers were a club, but not the Hell's Angels. They were retired Service Men of all branches who were now Business men, Lawyers, Doctors and such that got together each summer for a week or so to be buddies again and just unwind on their Bikes.

Dale X Phipps

Stock photo

Chapter 9

Lightning Fire on Old Baldy 1963

In the summer of 1963, our Ranger District had been hit with several lightning strikes. Most all the Naches District fire suppression crews were dispatched to fires all along Nelson Ridge around Mount Aix and Hindoo Creek. This left only Timber Management and Recreation personal available for back up.

As it turned out about daybreak the day after the lightning storm, the lookout on American Ridge (Goat Peak Lookout) called in a small fire on Old Baldy. Spike, our Ranger, chose me to take a green-horn Forester, Doug, on his first fire. Now there were several reasons Spike wanted me to take this fire. First it would take horses to get there. Second, Spike knew I knew the area because I spent 3 summers leading hikes over Old Baldy as a Boy Scout from Camp Fife. Third, I had a saddle horse and a pack horse. All but one old riding Forest Service horses was available, all others were out with the packers tending the fires on Nelson Ridge.

Doug and I had found the fire late in the afternoon. The fire was on the east side of Old Baldy at about 5,000 feet. We tied up the horses and went directly at putting the fire out. It was mostly one large old rotten conifer with a hollow center on fire. The ground under the tree had duff (forest litter) of almost 2 feet thick which was smoldering from partial burnt areas. We got out the cross-cut saw (no power saw) and went to work, cutting the old snag down, so we could break it up and put out the fire within it.

After the fire was out, we spent the next day watching for any hot spots or smoke. Not too much happened the second day, we carried water from a nearby creek and mixed it into the duff around the tree stump and the broken-up snag we had fallen, to be sure all flammable material was out. In the afternoon of the second day, it started to rain. The rain was God sent; it would be reassurance that our little fire would not reignite.

It was day three and the fire was out, and it was time to saddle up for home. While we were packing up my horses, Snooper and Lady along with the Forest Service horse Doug was riding, we could hear a distant rumbling. We thought it might be thunder; however, that was strange. It never seemed to quit rumbling. We continued to load the gear on Lady and the rain and rumbling persisted.

As soon as Doug was in the saddle, he hid himself in his rain coat atop his horse, as it was pouring rain. This left me and Snooper to lead the pack horse, Lady, and Doug on his F.S. horse down towards Thunder Creek

Trail. No big thing for Snooper, my horse and I, were better prepared for the lead, Doug being a GREEN cowboy. As we headed closer to the actual trail the roar and rumbling, we heard far off in the earlier saddling up time became even louder. Snooper found the actual trail in the down pour, I would have missed it in that heavy rain and fog, but he knew the way home. The rumble kept getting louder.

We were starting down into a steep creek crossing at about 4,000 feet. Snooper and I were about 50 feet from the creek bottom itself, when I looked back to see if Doug was still in the saddle, I saw he and his horse were about 30 feet behind with the pack horse in the middle. Also, as I looked back, I saw coming down Thunder Creek a massive wall of mud, logs, water, rocks as big as cars. The mud flow was at least 20 feet high and side to side of the total creek bottom. The mud and debris flow were moving faster than I could run.

I figured as close as the mud flow was to us, I and Snooper could make it across the creek and up the other steep side to safety, but Doug, Lady (my pack horse), and the F.S. horse would not. It was like Snooper and I got the same idea at the same time, with a quick jerk of the reins Snooper lunged around and headed back up out of the creek bottom. As we passed Lady, the pack horse we jerked her around and headed for Doug. He saw nothing; he was still hidden under his rain coat. I grabbed the head gear of the Forest Service horse that Doug was on and pulled it around. At this point Doug figured something was wrong and looked out of his rain gear to see the massive wall of debris coming at us. With a few more lunges Snooper had pretty much pulled all of us back up the hill to safety.

It took the mud flow about ten minutes to completely go by our location. We waited another hour to be sure nothing more was coming and cleaned our underpants and stopped trembling. Then because of the steepness of the hill side to the creek bottom, which was now straight up and down due to the slide, we had to build a new trail with our Pulaski's for the horses to be able to cross. It took well over two and a half hours to build a wide enough trail to safely bring the horses across the washout.

That was the longest 7-mile horse ride I would ever take. From the time we were packing up (7AM) till we got the horses loaded up at the Thunder Creek Trail head around 6PM. Cliff (F.S. Back Country Trail Crew Forman) was waiting for us with the Forest Service horse truck, he had waited at the trail head from around noon that day for that was the time we should have made it out. In those days Forest Service radios only worked on top of mountains, so no one knew what we had gone through till we reached the Ranger Station sometime around 9PM.

But for a quick powerful horse and a lot of luck we may never have been found. We were all hitched together in a rope line, so if one of us had been swept away we all would have gone together.

Chapter 10

Lightning Fire-Barton Creek 1964

The Naches Ranger District had been on a forest-wide shut down due to the extreme fire danger for over three weeks. All trails and off- road travel were stopped, and no camp fires were allowed outside of approved Campgrounds due to the fire danger. All Logging was also shut down, but first it had been on "Hoot-Owl" two weeks before this. Hoot-Owl is when it is so dry and hot that logging can only be done each day from sun-up till 1 PM. And now on top of the closures a large band of hot stormy lightning was coming up from Northern California. There were over three fires already in Northern California and Oregon was being hit by lightning around 1600 (4PM). With the direction of the twind and its speed, the prediction was we would have lightning by 2100 (9PM). At the time all we could do was wait and hope it would pass without strikes. The lightning hammered away for what seemed to be all night, but it was only for about 3 hours with ground strikes and 2+ hours with cloud-to-cloud bursts.

Next morning at daybreak all Naches District personnel were standing around in the compound near the gas pump waiting for orders. There was something new with the number of men on hand. Six strong young men from the Eagle Rock Saw Mill were there to give us a hand. In the 50s and 60s the Forest Service could hire any able-bodied man to help on a forest fire, "fire trained or not". Due to the Forest Fire closures the mill workers were out of logs to cut, so fighting fire would keep a paycheck coming in. It was quite common for young men from around the area to volunteer to fight fire, in fact it was one way some older high school boys could make good summer wages.

Things were pretty much at a standstill, until all the fire reports were in from the Forest Lookouts. Well, not all were standing still, Harry, the Fire Control Officer was all but running around in circles. Poor Harry, he was not so good at large complex workloads, and last night's lightning strikes made his world go upside down. Shortly thereafter Spike, the District Ranger and Packy his assistant, came into our group of standby men and began assigning who was to go to which fires. I was given the Mill crew as a team and our assignment was a ½ acre fire on the North side of Old Baldy in the Bumping. It was Spikes idea again with my experience of the Bumping drainage. It also helped that I knew all the men due to the fact I was the Timber Sales Officer for the Naches Ranger District and often checked their mill yard for our Forest logs to be sure they were properly branded before sawing.

On the way to the Bumping area, sitting in the shotgun seat, I looked over the map of the area to find the best way into our assigned fire. Now on the North West side of Old Baldy there is real heavy undergrowth and extremely steep ground with tightly grown second growth trees. Old fires and avalanches have made that north side of Baldy a mess and would be hard to climb through. There are no trails on that side of the mountain. When we got to the Bumping Dam, we drove to the north side so we could look back and see the smoke and approximately where our fire was. From what I could see, the fire was almost 2/3's of the way to the top of Baldy and not far in from an old avalanche and rock out crop called Barton Creek.

It was now time to put on our packs and carry whatever tools we could, shovels for some, "Pulaski's" for others. Pulaski has an ax head with a hoe opposite the ax, great for digging fire line. Two of the mill men thought they could manage carrying a small saw and gas, and of course I had that 26-pound portable radio. "Talk about a millstone over my shoulder."   Due to the thickness of the small trees and shrubs near where we started up the mountain, we decided to climb in the avalanche shoot. There were lots of loose rocks so my suggestion for the crew was each man should stay at least 50 feet behind the man in front of him so if a rock were jarred loose, they would have time to get out of the way of any falling rock.

It was a long hard climb and luckily, we all made it without any bad falls or lose rocks hitting anyone. The mill crew was doing quite well, they kept up with me all the way to the top end of the now smoldering fire. It was near midday and the temp was close to 90 degrees. I had the men sit down where ever they could and dig their heals in. The hill was so steep that when you sat down you were almost still standing. Before we arrived on the fire sometime around 10 AM., a crew of Smoke Jumpers had landed on the open ridge above the fire and had worked their way down to the fire itself. The jumpers had started a fire line on the right side of the fire "I'll call it the East side." After I had conferred with their foreman about where my crew should work, we decided that the left side or West side would be best, to stay out of each other's way on this steep hillside.

Things were going quite well I thought, most of the fire was on the ground and not burning high into the trees. Well, about 3 or 4 PM the wind started gusting and things got lively. Some of the Smoke Jumpers had started across the top of the fire with a fire trail. But they had to back off for the fire was running uphill towards them. I had my crew on alert for fire start-ups outside of our fire line, and to be safe and alert due to the steep ground things could change quickly and fire could be all around us.

I made a radio call to the Ranger Station to see if a "slurry drop," an air drop of fire retardant, was possible to help us hold this fire to only an acre in size. Packy answered that all retardant was directed to two Wenatchee fires that were up to 30 acres in size. His next question to me was," do you have any running water in a nearby creek?" At that time, I did not know, so I sent some of my crew in all directions to look for running water. Luck would be on our side -Young Simmons, one of my crew, found a small running stream about 100 yards north and west of the fire. I reported that to the Ranger Station and Packy said we would have a small plane drop, in an hour or two, with fire hoses and a sock. "Sock" a sleeve like canvas with one large end to scoop in water from a stream and the other end having coupling to hook fire hoses to. Even though the stream was small there would be enough water once nozzles were attached to the hose to make back pressure.

We could hear the roar of the small plane a few minutes before it flew overhead. Then I heard a crackle on my radio and Harry sputtered out "where do you want this hose?" I told him NW and two hundred feet from the fire. On the next pass of the small plane a hose came falling out of the sky, and 5 or 6 passes later more hose on each pass. The fire hose was 2 inch in diameter, in rolls of fifty feet. Each roll or coil of fire hose would weigh approximate 20 pounds. Thank God no one was in the area of his drop or they would have been crushed. After that I asked Harry or whoever was making drops to let us on the ground know in advance so we could get under a tree or completely out of the area.

By the time we had the sock in the creek and the hose down to the top end of the fire it was close to 8 PM. That hose and water made a difference. Now the fire was no longer trying to run uphill. After that we attached a split, a Y, and sent a fire hose down each side of the fire. The fire trails were holding the fire from spreading sideways, and with water sprayed into the burned areas would improve our chances of holding it in place.

That was one long day. There were two more drops that day, one with food and the second with bed rolls for the cold night ahead of us. You might think COLD? Its midsummer, but the crews and I were at 5000+ feet and the temperature change were going to be large. That day it had reached 94 degrees and that night was to be in the 40's.

Now sleeping was going to be a trick on that steep mountainside. But the Smoke Jumpers showed us a hillside ingenious method. They took their Pulaski's and dug a trench across the slope wide enough to lie in. The trench was also up against two or three trees on the down side, so you would not roll out. The trench worked great, we traded off every two hours watching the fire, half the crew slept while the other half watched for hot spots. We only had to dig half as many trenches and disturb much less ground.

The second day started out calm. With the fire surrounded and lots of water to help mop up the reaming hot spots, it was time for the smoke jumpers to pack up and leave. They needed to get back to their air base in Wenatchee and prepare for their next jump. Trucks would be waiting for them at the bottom of the mountain to take them back to their air base. This left the mill crew and me to finish putting out all fire hot spots.

WELL, some smart person back at the Ranger Station decided that we needed clean drinking water. (I think someone wanted to have an excuse to fly over the fire). Large tin-cans of about 5-gallon capacity were gathered up and filled with water. These tin-cans were about 12 inches by 12 inches by 18 inches high. The cans had a carrying handle brazed or welded to the center of the top of each can. A small parachute was attached to each can handle.

It must have been about 10 AM because we were all sitting down for a breather, when we heard Harry on the Forest Service radio. Harry said, "he had a delivery of fresh water, and where would be a good place to drop it?" This was a surprise to all of us, Water we had plenty. I radioed Harry that just above the highest point of the burned over area would be best. This was going to be a fun break from firefighting. I told the crew to watch for parachutes and we would retrieve them after all were down.

Suddenly as the little plane growled overhead a tin can of water came whistling through the trees. The water can crashed into limbs and bursting open with water and tin-can flying in all directions. Within seconds a second another water can came tumbling and screaming through the trees. I ran to my portable radio and pleaded with Harry to stop bombarding us with water cans. The parachutes were ripping off the cans due to the weight and the smallness of the parachutes. The cans were falling into the mid-section of the burn where most of the crew was at rest. Harry did not hear me on the radio, so on the next pass of the plane, two more water cans came whistling and crashing into our location. By then we were ready for the next water attack, everyone had found a large tree to get behind. I kept repeating on the radio to stop, but to no avail. On the third pass the pilot saw one of the water cans hit a big tree and burst without a parachute attached. That was the last of the water bombs and Harry and pilot left without an apology.

After all the excitement we went back to mopping up all the fire's hotspots. By the end of the day there was no more smoke or heat in the burned-out areas of our fire. We stayed one more day to be sure that no flames or smoke were present. On that third day we rolled up hoses and carried them to the top of the ridge so a helicopter could pick them up later.

On the fourth morning after the crew checked the fire area one last time, we gathered our tools and headed back down the rocky creek bed to our waiting trucks.

That was one of the best fires I had worked to date, no one got hurt and we kept the fire to less than 2 acres. When I say hurt that did not cover the blisters most all of us had on our feet. Due to the steep hillside we all were constantly digging our heels in, to keep from sliding. The odd pressure on our feet because of the steepness of the mountain moved our feet back and forth in our boots, no matter how tight we kept them. Sometimes you just cannot avoid a blister.

Chapter 11

In Memory of a Logger and Friend

In this short story I will probably wander from thoughts to old heartfelt memories of a young man whom I admired and loved like a brother even though I only knew him for two short years. Art was a "loggers' logger if you get my meaning. He could perform any of the many difficult tasks of the everyday life of a workman in the forest. Some People often think of a logger as someone who does not have many skills, someone who may be uncouth, lacking much of the world's knowledge. Well let me tell you with my 30+ years of working with these men of the forest and big trees they are quite skilled and some, if not many, are even college grads. Their reasons to work the forest and not the plush life of the city, are the freedom of movement, open space, and clean air plus many more subtle reasons I may get to as the story goes on.

I met Art in the spring of 1963. I believe it was on the Devil Creek Timber Sale, where I as the Timber Sale Officer was there to inspect the sale. Fred Webb owner of Webb Logging Co., himself told me that he was immensely proud and happy that Art was one of his top operators. Art had a degree in business that he earned while working through summers logging when he was a young man. Instead of following a career in business after collage he came back to the woods where he felt more at home. There was something about Art that when you talked with him, he was truly intent at listening to whatever the subject; logging, fishing, or whatever. He was one person in a million that you knew he was a friend at the start, and you could always count on his word. I only met his wife and children once, but the way he spoke of them then and later you knew they were a real team working together to make a better life for each of them. This was something I saw as a young man that was impressive. When we were not talking Timber Sale Contract, we talked about everything from hunting in the fall to old guns and family life.

Art was a Forman of one of 4 logging operations (sides) that Webb Logging Co. was operating on the National Forest in the 1950's through 1980. For the beginner, my first learning of logging, I will explain as best as I can what a logging side is. For the Webb Logging Co., a Logging side consisted of two fallers- men who fell designated trees; three cat (tractors) operators for one D-6 and 2 D-7 Caterpillar Tractors; two bushlers (men who cut trees at the landing into log lengths to be later loaded on to trucks); one Forman who operated the log loader; and a second loader man who, when not assisting on the log loader, operated the smaller D-6 Caterpillar tractor. The log loader was a converted Links Shovel. The Links Shovel was originally built to dig earth with a large bucket scoop. Fred Webb converted the shovels with large tongs to grapple logs off the end of the bucket, and later completely removed the bucket to make it easier to use the tongs in handling logs.

Loader and log truck-stock photo

With all this equipment there was also 4 to 6 log trucks and drivers assigned to each landing.   The first truck would show up at the landing (landing: the area trucks were loaded with logs) about 6AM, this truck would be loaded in 15+ minutes then head to Yakima and Boise Cascade Mill and arrive there around 8AM with the other trucks and drivers to follow at 15-to-20-minute intervals. Throughout the day trees would be fallen, tractors would skid (drag) the felled trees to the landing to be bucked into proper log lengths and bucked logs would be either stacked for later loading or "hot loaded" onto waiting trucks. Most log sides would produce 10 or more loads of logs per day depending on the size of the trees they were working with at the time. The Forman's main job was to make sure logs were bucked properly with defects removed; trees were felled in the direction of the landing to make it easier for trees to be skidded and less damage to the remaining standing trees; new landing sites were properly located in advance, machinery (saws-tractors-loader-trucks)were maintained; and the overall safety of his crew. On top of all that the logging on Forest Land had to be done by strict contract requirements, such as avoiding activity near streams; making skid trails as narrow as possible to preserve remaining standing trees, locating landings away from main roads and meadows; and trying to load out 10 or more loads of logs per day. The benefit of having ten or more loads was that the crew was paid a day's wage plus for each load of logs over 10 they all would receive a bonus. That part of being a Forman made things easy because they all helped each other produce. Easy except he had to make sure they were safe in their efforts to make the extra loads. Not becoming too tired and moving too quickly to cause harm to themselves or others. Working with saws and tractors and falling trees is a dangerous job and everyone on a crew must always be alert.

This would be Arts last day in the forest. It was clean up time for this site or landing and all the designated trees that would come into it were mostly removed. I had been requested by Webb to come to the site and check it out for completion. When I arrived at the site Art was loading the last truck of the morning with all sorts of left-over logs, from short stubby to thin long "pecker poles" (is what loggers called logs under 10 inches in diameter), and all other leftover logs as any clean up goes. Art hollered down to me from the shovel to go on out the main skid trail and check on the cleanup, he said he would catch up with me after he finished loading and helping the trucker tie down the load. It was customary for the loader man to help the trucker strap down loads of logs, for it was a dangerous job strapping cables on loose logs up to ten feet above their heads. By strapping with three cables approximate 6 feet apart on a load of logs it would become safe to move down the road and all logs would be tight and secure.

I was out in the logged area looking for missed felled trees or large enough broken pieces to make a small merchantable log (sellable log), for what seemed like over half an hour and Art never caught up to me as he said he would. I moved over maybe 200 feet and headed back to the landing on a different skid trail. When I hiked back into the landing everything was quiet, and the last truck was still sitting at its loading position. At first, I thought they, landing crew and trucker, were taking a break, but as I approached the log loaded truck, I saw why all was quiet. I saw Art lay on the ground not moving. I was told later that after the last pecker pole was loaded and Art had jumped down to help the driver wrap up; a log from the top of the load came free and started to roll off the load. Art saw the log coming off the load, but the driver did not. Art, without thinking of his own safety, dove forward pushing the driver under his truck and out of the way of the falling log. However, Art did not get clear, he took the blow of the falling log atop of his head. This was my worst day in the forest sitting in the dirt next to a friend Art,

waiting for the Coroner...
I attended his burial service June 24, 1964 at Terrace Heights Memorial Park.

Chapter 12

How Stag Found Me

It was late fall 1965, and after work I was on my way to feed my horses. The wife and I lived at the Naches Ranger Station, but my horses were pastured down near Rock Creek at the junction of HWY 410 on a small 2-acre pasture. Because the size of the pasture I had to supplement my horses with hay in the fall and winter, so every day I would drive down to Rock Creek to feed.

On my way down past the Pond Café I spotted a young medium size dog with a coat of hair color somewhere between a coyote and a wolf. The dog was trotting alongside of HWY 410 about 3 feet off the pavement headed East towards Squaw Rock store. At the time I thought one of my neighbors got a new dog and it was out looking the area over or had escaped his holdings. A few days later, on my way back to the Ranger Station somewhere between Squaw Rock store and the Pond Café, was a coyote-looking dog trotting west just off the pavement. This time I stopped and tried to call him to get him off the road. No luck-he headed straight away and up the hill just East of the Pond Cafe and into the trees.

It's now November a week or two later and it's snowing, and the temp is down in the 20's, I'm going down to feed the horses and there he is again on his way up the Hwy towards the Pond. After feeding the horses I make up my mind to try and talk to the dog again, I have seen him a couple other times between work and feeding drives up and down the 410 Hwy. As I approach the Pond Café, I spotted the dog sitting near the store's dumpster. I drive about 10 feet from him, and he is looking at me as though he could fight or flee. From the driver's seat I reach across the truck and open the passenger's door. The dog does not look like he wants company, but I talk to him. I talk to him, like I'm talking to a person and tell him to get in and I will find him his home and some food, and without any other words he climbed up into my old Dodge horse truck and sat on the passenger's side like he had been there before. I got out and closed my door and walked around the front of the truck watching to see if he would get out. He sat there and watched me walk around. I closed the passenger's door and went into the Pond Café. When I went into the store part of the Pond Café, Ruby "the store owner" was standing there saying she could not believe what she just saw. She told me she had been trying for weeks to get the dog to come to her, but no, he would just walk away. She had left food scraps out for him which he had consumed when she was out of reach. I bought a small bag of dog food that you put hot water on, and it makes a sort of gravy and it smells sort of meaty. I got back into the truck and he just sat there looking out the front window, so I drove to the Ranger Station and to my little F.S. rental house. I parked directly in front of the house leaving my truck door open, which faced the house, went in and made up the dog food with hot water. When I came out on the front porch with the bowl of food, I offered to him and held the door open for him to come in to the house. But he would not so I feed him on the porch. While he ate Bonnie, my wife, brought out water and a rug that she laid next to the door. We left him to eat and went inside to have our own dinner.

After our dinner we looked out and the dog was gone. So, I felt good that I had given him food and water hoping he would be OK and maybe even return.

The next day he was on the porch and it looked like he had rested on the rug, so I gave him more food and left the house to get my F.S. truck ready for the day of work. I did not know but Bonnie later told me that the dog had followed me to the edge of the truck shed and watched me leave in my F.S rig for work. After work and at home that night there was no sign of the elusive stray, however much later he showed up on the porch with a loud thud. He must have jumped over the stairs to the porch in one big jump. We brought him more food and fresh water which he ate and drank then left. Next morning it started all over again he ate and drank his food and water then follows me to my rig. This went on for two or three more days, till one morning as he followed me to the rig, I decided to name him and because of his hair color and his aloofness I called him **Stag**.(stag a male deer) After 5 days and nights of giving him food and water neither I nor Bonnie was ever allowed to be close enough to pet him, he would always move away if we tried to come close to him.

This was my Friday and was to be a short day in the Forest with office work in the afternoon, so as Stag and I got close to my rig I dropped the tail gate and told him to get in. With no hesitation he bounded up on to the truck bed and took his place up close to the cab on the left side with his front paws on the side railing like he had been riding there for years. Stag rode there for the next 11 years whenever I went to the Forest to do my job of Sale Administration.

There are many tales of what Stag and I did on and off the job which I will address in short stories as my time and memory allows.

With Stag in our early years ©K. Taylor

My pal Stag ©K Taylor

City Boy to Timber Beast

Chapter 13

Struck by a 32-foot Log

While Webb and I were talking by a landing fire in 1965 or 66, I was struck in the back by a swinging log. (Fred Webb the largest Logging Contractor on the Naches District.)

On a wintery day in the Devil Creek area, I and Fred Webb, were going over logging plans. We were on the edge of an active log loading Landing. Logs were being pulled by D-7 Caterpillar Tractors into the landing for bucking into desired log lengths, while a large crane (loggers called them shovels) was stacking the bucked logs in piles and loading trucks. The area we were standing in was where the buckers had a warming fire and sharpened their saws after each turn of logs were bucked. So, it normally was a safe place to be so close to the Loader swinging logs and tractors coming and going with turns of logs.

The job Forman who was the Loader man wanted to talk to us, so he called one of the Landing crew men to take his place. We had been talking for a short while, we all could see the second loader man was very nervous and making poor decisions on which logs should go where. So, the Foreman headed back to the Shovel.

Fred had his back to the loader, and I was facing it. Just then the nervous loader man pulled the wrong lever and the loader swung around in our direction with a large 32-foot log at about 4 feet off the ground coming fast. I yelled and pushed Mr. Webb to the ground. My instincts were to run. Why I do not know? So, I turned and started to run (I got about 6 feet) and the swinging log hit me belt high in the back. I was lifted off my feet and flung out into the forest. I must have been going fast enough when the log hit me, because I had no broken bones. However, lots of scratches and black and blue all over with a very sore back. I think Webb and his foreman were the first to get to me, they thought I would be dead or torn in half. But no, luck was on my side, and Webb was very thankful that I had pushed him down out of the way. There was a lot to talk about after that, but not much about logging. We were just thankful that both of us were OK. Well, except my back gave me trouble for several years. That is another story on how I relaxed it to tell later.

Here is my method of fixing the back pain: When my back would pop out of line from lifting or turning too fast, I would hobble on home. But the pain was wild up and down my back, and even if I stood straight or did not move sitting in my easy chair, I would feel extreme pain. I tried Aspirin, Tylenol, Aleve, even had the wife massage my back. Nothing worked.

One Friday night I was hurting so bad I took a double shot of Jim Bean went into the bed room and lay on my stomach. As the alcohol took affect I relaxed, and my back bones realigned and fell into place. There was a quick sharp pain down my back, and it was over, pain gone until the next time I moved wrong.

A few years later I had an accident with a horse I was training. It was way too early in spring; the snow had just left but ice patches were all around. While jogging around the corral the colts back legs slipped on ice and fell on its butt then it rolled over me before I could get out of the way. The weight of the colt and my foot still in the stirrup pulled my left leg out of the hip socket. I tried to stand but to my surprise my left foot was pointed to the rear and I had no strength in the leg. My wife and children were watching me from the house they immediately came out to help me up but could not. I told Bonnie (my wife) to unsaddle the colt and call for the Sherriff who lived just across the HWY and a short way up Rock Creek road from us. Vern, one of the Forest Service personnel, was visiting the Sherriff at the time so they both came to help. After that I had a rough 30-mile ride in the back of the local Sherriff's car to the hospital to have it rotated and pushed back in place.   When I healed up from that I had no more back aches. Because of the fall and crushing by the horse my back was made straight and sound again.

Loader and Log Truck ©Dale X Phipps

Chapter 14

Wild Rides in Helicopters

It was the summer of 1965 and the Naches Ranger District had suffered a major forest fire in the back country (Wilderness). Because of the steep terrain and the lack of roads, small Bell Helicopters were used to transport men and equipment to the fire. The fire was only mile and a half flight from Ravens Roost Lookout, and the Lookout had a Forest Service road to it. There was a large flat area on top of Ravens Roost, so men and equipment could be stored and shuttled as needed to the fire. This large flat area was created this same year to make room for construction of a microwave tower. The tower would handle Government and public phone service plus TV. This was an upgrade for the Northwest phone and TV service.

Now about the Helicopters that were available in 1965- they were small three-seat choppers as we called them.

The middle seat was the pilots' seat with one seat on either side of the pilot making it just two people at a time could be flown from Ravens Roost to the fire. Outside of the chopper were two baskets just above the landing struts to carry equipment. The Bell helicopter was the work horse for the Korean War, mainly used to transport injured soldiers and Officers to and from the front lines of battle. This little work horse worked great at elevations less than 4,000 feet, with a carrying capacity of 800 pounds. In those days, a super charged motor or blower was not available- which would have given more lift at higher elevations.

By now you may have gotten the picture that the little Bell Helicopters were not that safe at 6,000 feet which was the top landing area of the fire and Ravens Roost. Now I want you to picture this: Two men approximately 450 pounds, their equipment @ 200+ pounds all tied down in the baskets, add the pilot 200+ lbs. for a total of 850 lbs. or more, all this and trying to take off at 2,000 feet above their capacity. The takeoff was a Rube Goldberg experience. The little Bell Chopper would wind up all its power and hop and skip to the edge of the Ravens Roost platform and fall off the edge for about 300 to 400 feet before it acquired sufficient air to fly. If you were somewhere around the top of the Roost it would look like the Chopper was going to crash after falling off the landing area, then all of a sudden it would appear coming back up above the landing area and headed to the fire.

I only took one trip to the fire from Ravens Roost by Chopper. When my work was done at the fire some five days later, I put my pack on my back and took a 5-mile hike down to Hwy 410 for a safe pickup ride back to the Ranger Station.

The small Bell Helicopters were mostly used in Fire management, by moving men and equipment to remote fire locations. However, the Forest Service also used the Bell helicopter to locate other forest damage that may occur. The spraying of pesticides for the Woolly Aphid - the inspection of washed-out roads - grass seeding after a large forest burn in order to stabilize the soil – inspection of large areas of trees blown down. It was just one of those Blowdown areas that I and Ken T. surveyed from the air and estimated the volume on the Devils Table blow down in (1970 something).

How this was accomplished, first a ground crew completed measurements of several hundred trees on the ground in this area of all species-by doing this, a sample was made for the average tree size and volume.

Well, if you asked Ken or I at the time we would have said, we had the toughest job of sitting in the Helicopter counting trees as we passed over them for hours - LOL. Not so - it was at least it seemed to go on forever. The chopper pilot started flying us from one end of the blow down to the other end: then back to the other end by moving over on his rout about 200 feet from his last pass. Each pass was further up the hill side from the previous pass until the whole area was covered.

That was an awfully long day of counting trees that were blown down by a freak spring storm. The most interesting part of the day was not known for about two years. Through our counting and the timber crews measuring of the sample area, the cruse volume of the Blowdown

Timber Sale on Devils Ridge came within 15,000 feet of the actual timber removed. Now that was remarkable, most normal timber cruses only come within 50 or 100 thousand of the estimated volume cruised.

Bell Helicopter Stock Photo

On a hot summer day 1980 I was assigned to show a Huey Helicopter pilot direction to a small fire on the ridge to Little Bald Lookout. Now the Huey Choppers were the big thing in the 1980's, it was the work horse for the Vietnam War. It was bigger and more powerful than the little Bell Helicopters of the Korean Conflict that we used in the 1960's and 1970's. They were capable of haling 5 men and a crew boss to almost anywhere on the forest, provided there was a place to land it.

Huey Helicopter Stock Photo

Now on this trip in the Huey there were 5 fire fighters and their equipment, me and the pilot. The job was to find the fire and drop off the firemen as close to the fire as possible. It took us no time at all to find the fire. The crew as well as the pilot were anxious to set the chopper down so they could go to work on the small fire. As we (the pilot and I) looked around there were no clearings close by, only large trees close to the fire. However, there was a thicket of small Lodgepole Pine not 1,000 feet from the fires edge. I was looking further North and West of the fire for a landing spot. When suddenly, the chopper tipped up on its nose and headed towards the Lodge Pole thicket. I knew immediately what the pilot had in mind. The pilot was only a year at best from his service in Vietnam and I had seen pictures of the blades of flying choppers used to cut off brush in the jungles to make room for the chopper to land. I yelled at the top of my voice, "lift and do not run into the thicket of Lodgepole Pine." After we turned away from the thicket, I explained to the pilot that young Lodgepole Pine were not soft and supple like the bamboo and grasses of the jungle, they are hard as rock, and the blades of the chopper could not withstand the beating. We let the crew out in and opening about ½ mile uphill from the fire for a safe short walk back down to the fire.

Chapter 15

Young Tired Faller Hurt

It was midsummer and long working days, I as the Timber Sale Officer for the Naches Ranger District was on late day patrol looking for illegal fire wood cutters sometime after 18:00. In the 70's fire wood brought quick money to some who stole wood from the Forest, due to the need for cheap heating. Oil prices were sky high and stealing firewood after all the Rangers left the forest at 16:30 each night was quick and easy. However, I was on to their plan and that is why I was out there late.

Sometime around 19:00 I heard a saw in the distance, so off I went to check. As it turned out it was a faller by himself in a legal Timber Sale. He was what we call a bushler (a faller who cuts trees in advance of logging). He was totally by himself all others had gone home at 15:00 as they normally do, because they start at 4 to 5 AM. He told me he had taken a few days off earlier that week and needed the money, so he was working late to make up for his lost time. I had a bad feeling about him out there alone falling trees, and I could see he was tired. It was now pushing 20:00 (8PM) and I told him he should go home. He told me he was fine and would leave in about an hour. I left him but not feeling good about his situation. I spent another 2 hours driving up side roads looking for illegal firewood cutters before I headed back to the Ranger Station.

It was some time after midnight when I got a call at home from the Logging Boss of that Timber Sale where I had seen the Faller. The fallers' wife had called him because he had not come home, the Logging Boss knew I was out there that afternoon and questioned if I had seen him. Well, we put two and two together and figured he may have never left the site. I told the Boss where I had last seen him and that he did not look good -he looked tired at that time. Since I was closer to the area, I told the Logging Boss I would get dressed and head there ASAP. He said he would be close behind.

It took us till almost 4 AM to get back up to where I last saw the faller, and the head lights of the wood's crews were right behind us, so we had plenty of help to look for the faller. As daylight came, we found his parked truck where I had seen it the evening before. We rushed out to his cutting area in hopes he was alright (maybe he just laid down for a nap and did not wake up).

No, my Seventh Sense was right all along, we found him maybe 150 feet from where I last saw him. He was crushed under a tree that in falling it somehow fell backwards over him not away from him. His being tired and moving too fast he probably missed judged the lean of the tree and as it fell, he could not get out of the way. This was a terrible loss of life; I wish he would have gone home when I told him to.

Chapter 16

Horseback Trail Riding 1967

Since I started my career in 1959 on the Naches Ranger District, I had only worked under one Ranger, Spike, for eight years. There had been two assistant ranger changes and maybe 4 Foresters, but with only one head Ranger to follow his tone and ideas. Things were about to change as a new Ranger was in town. He was from eastern Oregon and was totally different in his leadership style.

First off, we had a district meeting with all personnel, Ranger Tom gave a quick over view of his ideas and where he wanted the district to go or improve. After the district meeting Tom took aside one by one the heads of all departments, I assume to learn their wants and needs, and their work loads and man power. When it came to my turn, we discussed the volume of timber removal I was checking on and anticipated problems. Things like safety of public use of active logging roads, fire requirements of contractors and such. Then out of the blue Tom asked if I had a saddle horse, which I think he already knew from talking to the other department heads. I said yes, and his next statement was a shock to me. He asked if I was available to check out a back-country trail with him? Somehow, I was his first pick to show off some of his new district to him. I guess really, I was his only pick, since I was the only horseman with my own horses on the Ranger District.

The investigation of the Backcountry of the Naches Ranger District started two weeks after the new Ranger arrived. Now these rides were not on weekends they were Wednesdays and sometimes they were two-day trips due to the length of the trail. Tom was determined to know his District so from mid-June through September 1967 we rode our horses on every backcountry trail on the District. Tom did not stop with just the trails, if he was not in a meeting on Tuesdays, he was traveling around the District with one of the other department heads-like the Engineering or Timber managers on one or more of District roads.

The first two Wednesdays were lowland trails that we traveled due to the snow in the higher elevations. July was different- the snow had retreated, and we were pushing the ridge tops of the Rattlesnake backcountry. After we conquered the Mt Aix trail, it was on to the Wilderness trails of Bumping River drainage. I had covered a lot of the District trails in my five years as a horse owner prior to Tom, but not anything like what we did that summer.

I should give you a little insight on the type of horseman

Tom was. He rode tall in the saddle and seemed to be ready for any unexpected varmint that might run out in front of us and spook our horses. But the one thing I could never get over was his horse. It was a well-built Quarter horse with lots of leg muscle and a well-shaped head. But it was an all-White gelding. Get it-a Ranger on a White horse? I gave him a lot of ribbing and asked him if he was a stand-in for The Lone Ranger on TV.

As the weeks and Wednesdays went by, we only had one horse trouble and it was on an overnight pack trip. We were moseying along the American Ridge trail on a hot August afternoon, and no words were spoken. We horseman and horses were kind of half off to sleep mesmerized by the rocking back and forth in the saddle and the warmth of the summer day, when out of the blue a branch that was pinned back as my saddle horse passed a tree close to the trail sprang free and slapped our pack horse in the head. It totally startled the horse which reared back and fell over on its back. How all this came about is still puzzling, but the horse was off balance by rearing and carrying the two pack saddles. She had one on each side of her and that helped pull her over on her back. The horse was upside down pinned there by two pack saddles - she tried to roll over but could not due to the packs on her back.

Horses are not built to lie on their backs with their legs straight up in the air because of the large cavity for food and heart and lungs etc. The horse may lay on its stomach or side. With the total back thing for any length of time the breathing will be pinched by the weight of the stomach and the heart will also suffer back-up problems in blood vessels. Bleeding from the nose and ears and suffocation can occur in a short time.

Tom and I were out of our saddles in a flash and running to the struggling horse. We tried to pull her to her side but could not due to those pack saddles. Tom grabbed my large, sheathed knife without asking for it and knew what to do. He cut the ropes that were holding the packs to the horses back and we pulled them away to give the horse wiggle room. Blood had already started coming from the horses' nose. Cutting the ropes and removing the packs was not enough – the mare still could not free herself. We each grabbed onto a leg-I a front leg and Tom a back leg, both on the same side of the horse. We pulled as hard as we could, and she began to pivot to one side. With a few quick lunges the pack horse was on her side and then standing. We let her stand there for over an hour. I brought her some water from a nearby creek.

Because of all that had just happened Tom and I decided to make camp close by and let the horses rest and eat. That way we also could watch the once fallen horse and let her inner body system fall back to normal and hopefully be alright.

About the pack Horse – she was the first horse I ever purchased. I named her Lady. I gave her that name because she was always spunky and a bit restless if I or any other man rode her, but if a girl or a woman came close to her or rode her, she was as gentle as a 20-year-old cat. Lady with a woman in the saddle would walk not run or trot and always alert not to harm the rider. However, if I came up to her too quickly, when she had no rider she would spook and run off.

Tom and I were close friends for the 3 and half years he was at Naches Ranger District. His wife's father became ill and they decided to return to Oregon to help run the family's large cattle ranch. With all the Rangers I have worked for on the Naches Ranger District his tenure was the shortest, but most enjoyable for me. I got to use my horses on the job!

Chapter 17

The Wolverine and I

This is another backcountry outing with Ranger Tom starting in October of 1967. We had set up an Elk Camp in Cement Basin over a period of 3 weekends. Cement Basin is on the Naches Ranger District and it is approximately six miles up the Union Creek trail from HWY 410, and less than one mile from the Pacific Crest Trail at about 6,600 feet. The camp was set up for all weather conditions such as a quick escape if a major snowstorm moved in while we were hunting.   First, we had hauled in by horseback: tents, cooking gear, and feed for the horses. There was time to find a safe area with plenty of water for man and beast all within a large tight clump of old growth trees to shelter us from wintery winds. Elk season always started in the first week of November, so we had to be ready for cold wet snowy weather especially at the elevation of our camp.

Finally, it was Saturday morning, the start of Elk season. The horses were fed, our breakfast eaten, and unused grub put away. It was going to be a great experience. We had fresh snow only about six inches deep which would make it great for tracking any Elk we may encounter. Our days hunting plan was to hunt alone and go in different directions, this would maximize our chances of crossing tracks or finding an Elk. Tom went Northwest out of camp and I traveled almost due North. My plan was to travel uphill all morning and then have a downhill return to camp in the afternoon.

I had been maybe ten minutes out of camp when a light fluffy snow fall began. It meant one or two steps then look each way due to the limited visibility caused by the falling snow. Moving slow and checking all directions continuously as you move is what you must do when hunting Elk. Elk are great at hearing different sounds and seeing movement-- it is their way to protect themselves. The falling snow also muffled any foot sounds I was making. It was a great day to hunt.

About an hour and a half out of camp I picked up on a lone set of Elk tracks, things were looking up. Cautiously I followed the track for what seemed like hours but was only 10 or 15 minutes. And there he was-a beautiful 6- point Bull Elk standing in a thicket of small Lodgepole Pine looking back at me. I froze and did not move a muscle, and wouldn't you know it my gun was at my side a long way from a shooting position. If I moved now, he would lunge off into the heavy forest without me getting a shot off. I had to wait till he looked away from me to take a quick shot. After what seemed like an hour, only 2 or 3 min, the Bull turned and looked away from me. My one shot was quick and deadly through the back of his neck. He did a half summersault and landed on his back.

The real work of hunting was when the butchering begins. Almost without thinking I ran down to where the Elk lay to remove his entrails and skin him out. By now it was afternoon, and I was up to my elbows in working this large animals' hide off him. There were no large trees nearby to string or hang the elk into so all the skinning had to be done on the ground. First cutting the hide from one side to the middle then turn it to trim the opposite side. Working with a 300+ lb. dead weight animal is no fun and doing it flat on the ground half at a time was difficult. His long legs I swear were still alive. They were always in my way and if I pinned one down to work around, it would come loose and bean me while I was bent over.

Thank God time passed, and the elk was free from its hide and entrails. I had also just removed the head, as I stepped back to marvel at my accomplishments, I was feeling totally drained of any strength from this day's work. Then out of the corner of my sweaty eyes I saw the meanest looking Cat-Dog? I had ever seen. It was slowly coming towards me and the now skinned elk. It was like the worst movie seen where all you see are the TEETH, HAIR, and EYEBALLS of a beast. Oh, and It had a growl that literarily ran chills up my back. I know if I had any left after all that work, I would have peed down my leg. I knew this thing did not want me. It wanted my elk. One more look at his teeth, his quick movements, and I knew it was time for me to leave. Without turning my back on it I picked up my gun and the Elk head and backed away till I was far enough away I could see neither the elk nor the Wolverine. Then I turned and headed for camp not knowing if I would ever see any of the Elk again.

Later back at camp when Tom arrived from his day's hunt, I told him of what had transpired, all the work I had done and then leaving in a hurry to avoid a bigger mess and possible injury. We decided to leave things alone that night and go back in the AM with the horses to pick up whatever may be left.

To our surprise the elk was not touched, not a tooth or claw mark. The hide still lay under the skinned carcass the only thing missing was the heart, liver and entrails. Other than the entrails this beast had good taste for delicate meats. We loaded up the elk onto my two horses and headed out of the area to avoid a second encounter with an angry Wolverine.

That was pretty much the end of Elk hunting in Cement Basin; as it turns out most, if not all elk, leave the very high country around the middle of October to head down to the feed stations. I guess all but the one I got. They are pampered elk, so they know when to head for free hay, supplied by the Washington State Game Department.

Wolverine ©Scott Shivley 2020

Chapter 18

Tree Kick-back at Rock Creek 1969

On an early afternoon in October 1969, I got a distress call on my CB that a faller was trapped under a tree in Rock Creek. I headed that way and met up with Steve, the local Sherriff to help him find the location of the accident. When we got there, we found all of O'Neal's fallen crew stand near the trapped faller. At first look he appeared OK no bleeding, his color was good, and he was talking. Here is what happened: the faller had cut the tree, it had fallen, and bounced up on its limbs then skidded back from the stump pinning him on his stomach against another tree.

Members of the crew were talking with him telling him that he was fine and as soon as they could get a front-end loader (a tractor with forks that lifts bucked logs onto trucks) up to where he was, they would lift the tree off him. He said he wanted someone to write down his last requests before the log was removed. Now to me and everyone else standing there that sounded odd. Except for old man O'Neal who immediately sat down next to the faller and pulled out his daily log cutting book to write on. The trapped faller started by saying to tell his wife and two young girls that he loved them, and that where ever he was going he would miss them. Then he went into where things were at home, like the keys to his truck were in his lunch pail, the insurance papers were with the house property papers, call his dad and tell him that everything will be OK and that he is not hurting. This went on for twenty + minutes, and then the front-end loader came crashing through the small trees nearby. All was quiet except for the tractor getting up next to the tree and its forks under its butt end some 10 feet away from the faller. As that end of the tree was supported by the tractor one of the fallers cut the butt end of the tree about 30 feet away from the pinned faller, which made it lighter so lifting it away would do no more damage to the downed man.

Then again all was quiet, and we all said a prayer with the faller as he had requested. The tractor fired up and gently lifted the log away from him. As this was happening, he was holding the hand of Mr. O'Neal and talking or maybe another prayer together. For a few minutes after the tree was pulled back and it would appear, he was going to be OK, he thanked everyone and looked as if he were trying to get up but fell over and was dead. We tried to revive him with all the CPR we knew, but evidently, he was too badly broken up inside to survive.

Tree Faller cutting tree ©Dale X Phipps

Chapter 19

Big Bald Mtn Lookout Storm-July 1970

It all began about midday in late July of 1970, with an exceptionally large lightning storm headed our way at the Naches Ranger District. The storm had come in from the Pacific Ocean and entered Northern California, leaving three fires in less than one hours' time. By 2:30P.M. the weather had moved the storm into Oregon and moving North to Washington. Before the lightning storm arrived in Washington it was able to ignite 8 more fires, that was eleven fires, and this storm was still building steam headed towards the Naches Ranger District.

About 6 PM (1800), Gordon, our Fire Control Officer, was assigning personnel areas to go to and wait for the lightning to arrive. He spread out all but one crew to areas on high spots to watch and be ready to take on any fires that may happen near their location. The one crew he had held back was for backup, so if one of the crew's possible fires turned out to be more than they could handle the backup could head out and assist.

By 6:45 PM the Lightning was occurring all around the District. Since I was at the office on standby Gordon sent me to head up to Big Bald Mountain Lookout. That Lookout had not been occupied for some time but being extremely high and mostly in the middle of the Ranger District it would make an excellent spot to view the District during the storm.

It was going to take me an hour and a half of hard driving on unimproved Forest roads. I strapped myself in and headed off in my trusty 1969 4x4 Chevy F.S. truck. I had been driving for almost an hour and the lightning was all about the area I was driving into. I was on what we call Rocky Prairie with about 2+ miles to go to Big Bald Mountain Lookout. Things were first dark then bright as the lightning flashed overhead and the wind picked up. Things felt kind of eerie with the air charged with electricity, large bangs and rumbling from the storm. The fact was I was wondering why I was there and what would happen next. Driving as fast as I could on the dirt and rocky road now somewhat wet due to a light rain becoming muddy with pelting hail and rain.

Then it happened, about 300 feet directly ahead of me a bolt of lightning struck a tall Douglas fir. The light was blinding and almost before and during the strike the CRASHING ROAR made me tremble and deaf for maybe 5+ minutes after the strike. I had slammed on the breaks (thank God) because the tree was torn apart with limbs and wood flying everywhere. A minute or so later I pulled myself together and put the Chev PU 4x4 into 4-wheel drive then drove genteelly up the road over the branches, bark and large chunks of wood to where the tree once stood. What I found, of what was once a 100-foot-tall and 30 inches in diameter at the stump Douglas fir was now a pole of 4 inches at the stump and only 20 feet tall. There were no signs of fire only destruction of a healthy Douglas fir that had been in the wrong place at the wrong time. I had never seen a tree struck with lightning that turned out that way before or since. It must have been some sort of mineral in the soil under that tree to have that happen.?

Well, the storm was not over so, I continued my way to the lookout and an evening of natural God given Fireworks (lightning flashing, thunder roars, hail drops as big as baseballs crashing onto the lookout roof). The storm on our District lasted almost till midnight. From the lookout I spotted 4 fires that night. Crews were dispatched to put them out quickly before they became dangerous large wild fires. I stayed at the lookout till daylight to make sure no more fires popped up that I may have missed during the storm.

The next morning on my way back to the District Office I stopped and removed limbs, bark and wood chunks from the road. What I could make out was that the lightning had struck the tree at its top and spiraled down to the ground, kind of unwinding it to its center core. It had tossed its bark, limbs, and wood core in 360 degrees all about its stump. The broken and shredded tree parts were thrown up to 300 feet in all directions. Again?? It is amazing what nature can do.

City Boy to Timber Beast

Chapter 20

Ravens Roost and Fifes Ridge Almost-Fire

Now this will be a tale to cover all my tales. It all started one mid-July Sunday evening. I and Glenn were designated to watch our children while our wives were at a baby shower. Glenn had been on the District for almost 3 years, but never really had a chance to see much of the Forest. Glenn oversaw reforestation, which was the replanting of trees in burned over areas or openings caused by logging. For the most part these areas were less than 3500 feet in height. You do not get to see much down in the depth of the forest. So, to keep our kids calm and give him a chance to see some of the area we headed out in his car for Ravens Roost which is 6,100 feet.

Ravens Roost was a major Lookout in the 1920s through 1960, due to its height and location. From where the old lookout stood you could see most of the northwest of the Naches Ranger District, except of course, the creek and river bottoms hidden deep in the mountains.

It was a nice slow drive up from the junction of the Little Naches River and Crow Creek campground, 17 miles to Ravens Roost. The kids were quiet, and Glenn got to see some of our reforestation of the 1960s in the lower reaches of Crow Creek. We reached the lookout about ½ hour before dark and watched the sun set.

Now on our way up we passed several wayside camps (people just setting up camp in any opening) and the smell of camp fire burning made us both nervous. We were nervous of so many camp fires and summer coming on hot and dry. Most of the campfire wood being burned smelled of Ponderosa Pine or the old standby and easy to get White Fir. There is lot of dead and down White Fir in the Crow Creek area.

We stayed on the top of Ravens Roost till I would say 10PM or so, then gathered up our children and started down. But just before we got back into the car, we could smell a sweet pine smoke that only comes from White Pine. White Pine is high elevation species that only grows over 4,500 feet. We had not seen any camps up high on the mountain-they were mostly in the first 5 or 6 miles along the Ravens Roost road.

I know I keep talking about smoke, but in summer it is always on our mind (if you are a Forester) that someone will leave a campfire and start an unnecessary forest fire. Forest fires also are started from lightning and we did have a small storm a week back. Lightning fires do not always show up immediately after a strike, sometimes they creep around in the duff and roots of dead trees for weeks before they openly become blaze.

Glenn had driven about one mile down the switch backs off the mountain, when to the south and east at about 5 miles away we could see fire. The fire was bright yellow and white flashes as though the flames had come in contact with many dead trees and brush. This all fit together: the smell of White Pine burning and now visible fire at an elevation of over 5,000 ft. We were truly not prepared to do an accurate job of locating a fire. A fireman's map from his glove compartment of the District and the bends in the road kind of lined us up with the direction of the blaze. The fire had to be on Fifes Ridge east of Hall Creek and mostly on the south side of that ridge.

We did not have a Forest Service Radio because we were in Glenn's private car, so all we could do was head back to the Ranger Station. Before we left our advantage spot, we could see the fire rise and flicker bright white and rolling between trees on the ridge top. After a harried trip off the mountain Glenn dropped me off at the office while he took the kids home to my place and his. I contacted Smokey, our Fire Control Officer, and brought him up to date on what we had found.

Because the fire area was all on steep ground and in the middle of the night, it was decided to wait until morning to go after this fire. It was shortly after 6AM Monday morning and Rexford had summoned up 8 fire fighters ready with packs. Glenn was to take 4 and head up Hall Creek from HWY 410, I and the other 4 men would try to access the fire from Crow Creek. Either way it was going to be a hard climb to our fires site. By 7:30 AM both our crews were on their way up Fifes Ridge and what we hoped was a small fire. In the meantime, Smokey sent a crewman up to our last night's location to observe the fire and report our progress.

It was sometime between 10 and 11 AM when my crew made it to Fifes Ridge top and about the same time Glenn and his crew reported they had reached the top of the ridge. As best as we could tell we were about ¾ to a mile apart on the ridge. No one had seen fire or smelled smoke. Glenn radioed he was going on up the ridge with his crew in search of fire and that I should close the gap between where our crews had reached the top. About the same time a radio call came in from the crewman sent to our last night location could not see flames or smoke. This was troubling. There was lots of fire last night there should be at least smoke?

Glenn and I and our two crews spent the rest of the day marching up and down Fifes Ridge looking for the fire. There was no fire to be found. We hiked and looked and smelled for smoke till it was almost too late to safely get down off the ridge to our rigs and return to the station.

So, what did Glenn and I see Sunday night? It was bright it moved up and down through the trees. There were flair-ups then almost no fire then bright and flashing fire between trees.

On our way back to the station all Glenn and I could do was question our vision of Sunday night. At the same time Rexford back at the station was checking the night photos from space. In the early 1970s the Forest Service had access to military satellites over the US to look for fires that may be started by man or Lightning. Now the night photos were great to pick out fires so that is what he was checking with the help of military experts. We never got to see the photos we were just given the location of possible fires. As it turned out there were small camp fires up and down HWY 410 and in the Crow Creek drainage, but none on Fifes Ridge.??

Did we see something further away than 5 miles? Yes, we did. The US Army was having night maneuvers at the Yakima Firing center. In this type of night Army game flairs are shot into the sky to light up the movement on the battle field. The flairs used for this type of night maneuvers are on a parachute to keep them suspended for several minutes and they float up and down depending on the air flow at the time. What we saw was the glow of the flares through the trees on the ridge top. From our position on Ravens Roost, we never saw the full shape of the flare only a glare and burst of bright light through the ridge top trees.

This was without a doubt the longest and hardest Goose Chase I have ever been on, and I started it myself.

City Boy to Timber Beast

Chapter 21

Injury to lone tree faller 1978

It all started on a Spring Sunday morning. My children and I had been to Naches for 9:30 Mass at St. Johns and then a bit of quick grocery shopping at the Naches market. By the time we got back to our home on Chinook Pass, it must have been close to 11 AM. We were unloading the car and removing our church clothes when I heard a short call on the Boise Cascade radio. Did not hear what was said. My Scanner could hear calls from Boise Cascade, Layman Logging, Zwight Logging, Jefferson Logging, Webb Logging and Beattie and Sanger Logging only, but I could not send calls.

In my days as a Timber Sales Administrator on the Naches Ranger District I had purchased scanner radios, one for the house at home and one for my F.S. truck. I was responsible for all the large timber sales on the District.

The job covered as many as 5 sales at one time. There were new spur roads to check; log trucks to look over for fire tool requirements; timber sale boundaries inspections to be sure no one crossed into another sale; checks for utilization of timber; you name it, I had to check it. Most timber sales that were being logged had as many as 6 men working at one time. Then there were at least 3 trucks and drivers making 2 to 3 trips a day with logs headed to Naches or Yakima. I found out early on in my career that a Scanner Radio and a CB radio would connect me faster to a problem then finding out the next day after a problem had happened.

Some logging operators such as Webb Logging, Zwight Logging, Beattie and Sanger Logging, and Jefferson would from time to time pick up their radio mike and just say "I sure hope Phipps comes by today. I have this problem ....and want his advice." If I heard the call, I could then head their way and call one of their truckers on my CB to have them call the boss to let him know I was coming. This would help in other ways; sometimes I may be headed towards the farthest part of the District to inspect a sale or a close one but would hear on their radios that the logging side was shut down due to one reason or another. I would then change my directions and head to an active logging site saving me lots of time and miles.

Back to what I was hearing on my scanner: after a minute or two I heard a loud call from a frightened man calling for help. Now I did not know where he was or who he was, but he did sound as though he was in distress. I froze in my living room; I had to stay and listen. Who was calling and from where on the Boise Cascade radio? Two minutes later with the next call, the voice was lower and said, "I'm in the Cheney Ranch area and have cut myself and need help, don't anyone hear me?" <u>Well, no one answered</u>. It was Sunday and everyone, but that faller was home away from radios. As quick as I could, I called George (Jeff is his nick name) and reached him after first calling his home then his shop. As it worked out Jeff and some of his racing crew were working on their race car. I told him of the calls I was hearing, and I was most sure it was one of his fallers who had cut himself and needed help. I am sure the faller was trying to get a few extra trees on the ground for the next day of logging.

Jeff told me he and the men at his shop would head that way to give as much assistance as they could and radio the faller that he was coming. I told Jeff I would call for an ambulance and the local Sheriff to direct the ambulance. It would be impossible to explain to an ambulance driver how to drive up the Rock Creek road then the Cheney road then a small dirt spur to where the faller was.

What had brought us to this point was that a lone faller had slipped and fallen on his power saw while the saw was running. He had received a massive gash to his left arm. (Needless to say, that a power saw on human flesh will not be pleasant to look at.) The faller had wrapped his arm as best as he could, and then made his way to the landing site. At the landing there was a log loader which had a Jefferson and Boise Cascade radio.

It was kind if eerie waiting for more talk on the radio. I had heard the Sheriff talk to his base and Jeff try to make a call to the faller, with no response from the faller. About 30 minutes had passed and finally I heard the Sheriff call his station to say that he was leading the ambulance up Cheney road. Shortly after Jeff came on the Boise radio franticly calling for the Sheriff and Ambulance to get there. Jeff was so upset that he did not realize that the Sheriff could not hear him on a Boise radio. More time went by and finally Jeff came on the radio and said the faller was on his way to town. He was alive.

Later, the next time I contacted the Jefferson crew I found out that the faller had lost a lot of blood and cut almost ½ way through his arm. The faller knew he was too weak to drive and his only way to receive help was through the radio.

Up until this accident a lot of the loggers really did not want me listening in on their company radios. But like I told those who had told their unhappy views to me, about my being able to listen on their radio systems. "If you're not doing anything wrong what's the problem?" So now for many of those doubters it was a good idea that I may help more than myself, even 'someone else' -**maybe even one of them**.

Chapter 22

The Bears and I

Black Bear ©Dale X Phipps

Over my last 60 years of work and play in the National Forest I have had 7 close encounters with the North American Black Bear. With all these encounters I still like to see them and admire their quiet and swift movement, even though they look big and clumsy, they are not.

Bear #1: My first meeting with a bear was in 1956 and it happened at Camp Fife. Camp Fife is a Boy Scout Camp in the Bumping River drainage of the Naches Ranger District. I was an archery instructor, and my archery range was at the very back of the camp. The range was far enough away from all other Scouting activity to make it safe from a possible misfired arrow. Also, to ensure that things were safe my personal tent and camping gear were at the range, so when there was no activity, I could keep an eye on the equipment and out of reach of adolescent boys.

The night of the encounter I and the staff were having a meeting about 9:30 PM at the main lodge. This was after having a Council Fire for all the scouts in camp that week. Now I guess I am getting ahead of myself; I should tell you of the bear a bit. My tent was more than 200 yards north of the lodge and a quiet place at night and away from all the Boy Scout camp sites. Also, behind the archery range and close to my tent was a well-used game (animal) trail off the mountain. and down towards the lodge and cook shack. I used this same trail to go to and from my tent and the rest of the camp. Needless to say, a bear would often make his rounds by my tent at night on his way to the cook shack and the garbage cans. I had heard him pass by several times and I know he knew I was in the tent, because he surely heard and smelled my presence while I was either sleeping or working at fixing broken arrows from that day's activity.

After the meeting I headed up the trail without a light. It was a moon-lit night, I knew the trail by heart- it had only a couple of hard turns but was mostly straight. Well, of course, like most 16-year-old boys I was either running or at a fast jog back to my camp and about halfway there was one of those sharp hard turns. I went around the big Douglas fir that was the reason for the hard turn. I went into a dark spot shaded by the tree from the moon, and BAM I ran face first into the back of the bear. I squealed and it grunted and we both went in different directions. I ran back to the lodge I think before I could catch my breath. Some of the staff were still in the lodge and they could see I was kind of shook up. The staff that was there could see 2-inch-long black hair on my white camp shirt and without much of a story from me they knew what had happened. It took me most of an hour before I could talk myself into going back up the hill to my tent. This time with my flash light on I headed back to my tent.

Bear #2: In the summer of 1964 I was working on two different timber sales which were not more than 5 miles apart. In the morning I had made logging contract inspections on the Swamp Creek timber sale and after that drove to the Lindsay Camp sale. It was after one PM when I arrived at a road junction where the log truck drivers were to mark their logs before leaving the forest. I decided to eat my lunch there. It was a great spot to watch for animals in the meadow below the road junction and check on the truck drivers to see if they were marking all logs as required. Now in those days a Forest Service truck did not have air-conditioning, so both my side windows were rolled down to get as much outside air as possible. On several days in the past month, I had observed deer and an elk or two eating or just passing through the meadow. Things were quiet this day. After over 20+ minutes there had been no trucks and the meadow had shown no life either. After completing my first sandwich I turned to the right to get into my lunch pail for another. Guess who was looking in my passenger side window not 4 feet from me and closer to my pail then me? YEP, it was a small bear maybe a two-year-old standing on his back legs looking in my open side window. I think before I turned in my seat, he may have been ready to reach in to the lunch bucket. Because my turning which startled him, he pushed off from the side of my truck and was gone in a flash into the forest. Now would not you know it shortly after the bear left a log truck and load of logs rolled up to the log marking area? I climbed out of my rig and started up a conversation with the driver, telling him what had just happened. He was not too impressed. I think he thought I was making it up.

Bear #3: The summer of 2004 I was new at searching for the Northern Spotted Owl and had the opportunity to have two young people help me search. My Granddaughter Brianna and her friend Danielle were out of school for the summer and were spending time with my wife and me. It was a great thing for me and the girls to get out of the city and explore the forest plus help me look for owls. On this day we were in the Dead Horse Owl site, and this was my first time in that area. The three of us had been searching from 9AM and it was now a little after 1PM when we found a flat spot and decided to sit down and have our lunch. Shortly after we set down, we heard voices coming from above our location. As it turned out in our crisscross search, we ended up close to the Fife's Ridge trail. So not to frighten the people going by just out of sight from us we sat silent. Looking at each other almost laughing to think how close we were to these people and they did not see or know we were there. Shortly after the hikers passed our position, Danielle let out a short high-pitched peep. Brianna and I turned to see what her little squeak was all about, and there not 10 feet from Danielle was a yearling cub bear. When Brianna and I turned to look in Danielle's direction our motion spooked the cub and ZAP he was gone in a flash. My best guess is that the bear must have been on the trail above us and the hikers surprised it and it slipped down off the trail in our direction to avoid them only to be surprised again by us. I bet that little bear never got close to another human again in its life.

Bear #4: The year was 2005. Every time I tell this story I get a chuckle. I was on my daily search for the Spotted Owl and this day I was in the Milk Pond area. The day had gone well I had found a pair of (NSO) Northern Spotted Owl's and the female was on a nest. I gave the male a couple of mice to be sure where the nest was located. By giving the male a mouse he in turn would bring the mouse to the nest for the female, this made locating the nesting owl much easier to find. When a nesting owl is found one should not spend too much time near that area to avoid upsetting the nesting bird and maybe losing the new owlets, so I packed up my gear and headed out.

When I crossed Milk Creek the rush of the water covered up the sound of my foot steps and the breeze if there was one must have been hitting me in the face, because just a few steps away from the creek I could hear snapping and cracking of small tree limbs. My first thought was I had frightened a deer or elk that had been at the creek to drink and it was making a fast get a way through small trees to my left. I stopped to check out the noise which seemed to continue and not go away- the sounds were still strong. To my left and up a steep hillside were many small trees which made it impossible to see what was going on in them or just beyond them. For a moment, the clicking and snapping stopped, and then a rapid cracking and snapping of small limbs started up. Almost as fast as it started it stopped with the sound of a THUD! And out of the thicket of trees, rolled up in a ball, came a bear. When the rolling bear reached the flat area at the bottom of the hill where I was standing it stopped rolling and straightened itself out. The bear got up on all fours his head hung low not looking in my direction and slowly walked away. It was like he was embarrassed and was turning his head away from me not to make eye contact, acting like nothing happened.

After the bear was out of sight, I had to see what made all the snapping and then crashing sounds I had heard. I retraced his descent direction and found a fast-growing Douglas fir of about 18 inches in diameter at the stump and only maybe 30 feet tall. It was 8 inches diameter where most of its limbs were stripped off. The bear had tried to climb the nearest tree to hide from me, but there were no larger trees, so he took this one. Because the tree was young the bark was thin, and his toe nails had only a ½ inch thick, soft bark to grasp on to. When the bear stopped climbing at the 8-inch diameter mark and the thin, soft bark gave way and he rapidly slid all the way back down to the ground. He was so embarrassed. This time there was no hurry, he just walked away.

Bear #5: The year was 2006 I was in the Scatter Creek drainage of the Naches Ranger District looking for three known Spotted Owl nest sites. I had never been to this area before; other forest wildlife people had always checked it out before this year. It was early enough in the spring that there were small patches of snow in shaded areas so travel over the forested land was slow. Besides the snow and wet slippery soil on steep slopes I had to search for trail markings. This first site I was looking for was originally found in 1994, now that was12 years ago and the small orange paint dots left by the founders of the site were fading and difficult to find. To top off all my troubles for this day the wind had come up about a half hour after I left my rig to search for the Scatter Creek site of 1994. Because of the snow, slippery steep slopes, wind, and poor trail marking I was not moving fast or making very much noise (if any noise it was covered by the wind).

After about an hour of searching I was cold and tired and decided to rest a while out of the wind behind a large Cedar tree which was just ahead of me. The tree had a very faint paint mark and would be a good spot to rest behind and visually scan for the next mark. As I rounded this huge old tree, I came face to face with my first light brown bear. It was hiding from the wind and because of the wind could not hear me approach. I have seen many a black or dark brown but never a tan bear. We must have been within three feet of each other before it spun around and headed up a steep wet, slippery slope. Now this bear had to be over 6 feet tall if standing erect and weigh over 200 lbs., but in a flash, it went straight up the hill at a speed I could not go downhill on a good day. In the bears way there were downed trees, snow patches, and a slippery wet slope. Within that flash he had traveled over a hundred yards and out of my sight and making no sound. Now I know the wind did muffle some of the possible sound, but the bear was jumping up onto one tree then down to the ground then up on another downed tree and all I heard was the wind passing my ears. Boy can they move and do it quietly. No wonder you hardly ever see one.

Bear #6: the year was 2011.   I was headed into the South Fork of Quartz Creek to a nest site I had been to many times, and as always, I was taking the shortest route straight up the hill from the road. The trails to most of the Spotted Owl sites usually meander along game trails which are great for walks in the woods. But walks are not what I do, I am trying to get to as many Owl sites in a summer season as I can and cover each site 3 times to be sure of their occupancy. On this short cut it was straight up a hill for maybe 300 yards then a flat bench for 50+ yards then up another lesser hill to the nest site.

I had just climbed the first hill to the bench and rested a minute not really looking around and just pushed forward into the flat area. I heard rustling of branches which I though may have been from a deer or elk that had been eating or sleeping on the bench ahead of me. Then as I moved even further across the flat, I heard Pine bark being scratched in frantic rapidity. Then out of the corner of my eye to my left I saw two cub bears frantically climbing a large smooth barked Pine tree. Now I knew these little guys were not alone. Quickly I searched my surroundings for their mother. She had to be close by. Almost out of nowhere about one hundred feet to my right she appeared, by standing up from behind small 4 or 5-foot-tall new growth trees. She looked to be 7 feet tall (but you know how the mind plays with you) maybe she was 5 feet tall. But the real point was I was between her and her cubs. (NOT A GOOD PLACE). Putting together all my knowledge and the tales of other people's forest experiences with bears, I decided to move backwards. Not taking my eyes off the sow I lifted my arms with my pack in my hands to make me look taller and bigger. Slowly stepping backwards as to not stumble and fall, still watching what the mother bear was doing. I moved to the brink of the hill I had previously climbed and as soon as I knew I was out of her sight turned and went downhill. After some distance I then stopped to look back to see if she was following, no she was not. -WOW - that was a close one.

Bear #7: The year was 2015. In the Miriam Creek drainage of the Naches Ranger District, I walked up on this bear. This field trip was early in the Spring and the Winter's snow was still a foot deep in places. It was sometime around noon and I had just visited the Spotted

Owl pair at the Miriam site. Things were going great. I found the male S.O., given him a mouse, and in turn he led me to the female and their new nest. After taking several pictures of the new site and the male Spotted Owl, I marked a new trail (paint marks on trees) out to the old main trail of last year's nest which would then lead out to the forest road. As I walked down a dry creek bed mostly covered in a blanket of old soft snow, there before me were bear tracks.

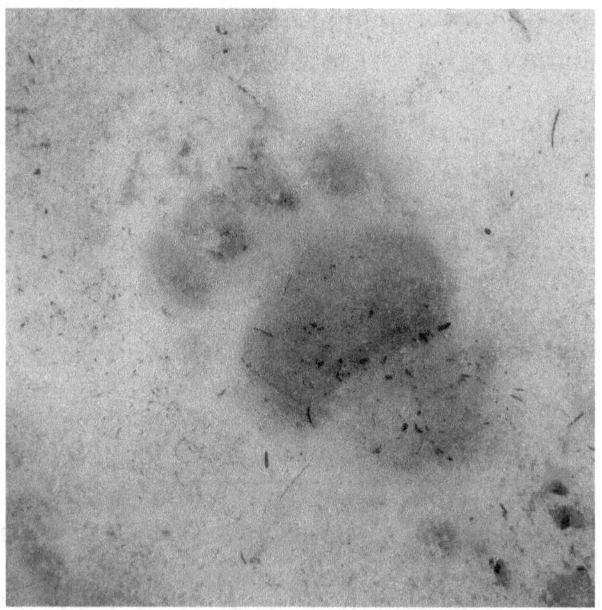

Bear Tracks ©Dale X Phipps

The tracks were not there when I had gone up the creek in the morning and they were quite fresh. I grabbed my camera from my belt camera holster and took several pictures of the prints. Then turning to start down the trail again I spotted the bear. He was probably 100 feet + from me with his back to me.

Bear sunning himself ©Dale X Phipps

My camera was still in my hand from taking the foot print pictures, so I took a picture of the bears back side. Then I realized what he was doing, he was sunning himself. The bear was just out from the tree cover and standing in the open meadow. He was swaying from side to side as the sun beat down on his head and back. That was probably his first warm day out from Winter hibernation. After watching him sun himself for what seemed like 10 minutes probably only 2 minutes, I aimed my camera one more time at his back end and shouted at him. The bear spun around almost exactly 180 degrees landing in the direction of me, one quick look at the shouter (me) and he made another quick turn, and he was gone. By the time I lowered the camera I never saw him cross the meadow of only 40 or 50 yards and into the tree on the far side.

Once again, a bear is gone in a flash and no sound.

Black Bear ©Dale X Phipps

Chapter 23

Using Boy Scout First Aid Training

In the early spring of 1978, I was on an inspection of the Benton Creek Timber Sale. It was particularly important that I complete a thorough inspection due to the fact this sale was being logged by a new logger from the city of CleElum. As it turned Boise Cascade had moved Webb Logging to Boise Idaho to do some long line skidding since Webb was the only logger, they had that knew that type of logging. Taylor Logging and Beattie and Sanger were Webb's replacement in the Yakima area. For this sale in Benton Creek Taylor Logging was chosen.

Personally, I knew nothing of the Taylor personnel and their operating practices, so all facets of the falling and bucking of marked trees, tractor skidding of logs, loading logs to trucks headed for the Yakima Boise mill- had to be checked out to see if they were in compliance with the

Timber Sale contract.

After looking over the log loading operation I headed out into the area of the tree fallers. Now the fallers for the Taylor Logging Co. were a separate contractor by the name of O'Neill Fallers. I found the falling Forman and we were talking over faller fire requirements, i.e.: fire extinguisher and shovel within 50 feet of their work. When out of the blue a whistle came through over the sounds of power saws.

Now the O'Neill fallers all carry a tin whistle like a referee or police man would have in order to signal one another of danger or someone needing help. The Forman and I stopped talking, hesitated for a short second and then we both headed towards the tweeting whistle. We had headed straight to the whistle sound - which took us over and through newly fallen timber, but within a few minutes we were at the faller's location.

What had happened was the faller was bucking (cutting) limbs off a fresh fallen tree, when somehow the tip of the saw blade jumped from the limb he was cutting and into his boot. A power saw at full throttle cuts very fast, before he could shut off or redirect the saw his foot was cut just below the ankle. He had blown his whistle immediately knowing he was in trouble and would need help getting first aid and to a hospital.

By now other fallers were with us looking over the situation. I knew we needed to get his foot out of the boot as quickly as possible. There was plenty of blood and the rest of the foot would swell making the removal more difficult if we waited. After unlacing the boot one faller began to pull the boot off, but flesh from the cut protruded up through saw cut hole. I quickly tucked the protruding flesh down into the boot so it would pass the cut area without more damage to the foot.

The bleeding continued even with direct pressure on the wound. The cut was about 3 inches across and at the deepest point ½ to ¾ inch deep through bone and flesh. We needed a tourniquet and we needed it fast. No one had a first aid kit nearby-only up at the log landing, and what I could see was that would take too long to go after and return. The only thing I could think of was my T-shirt. It was fresh and clean this morning. I took off my coat and shirt I pulled off the T-shirt. Taking hold of one side of the bottom of the shirt and the opposite side near the neck I twirled the shirt into a foot and a half long 3-inch-wide bandage. By pressure wrapping the cut area and tying a half hitch knot on the underside of the foot, most of the bleeding stopped. Asking the fallers to find a stick to help tighten the pressure, I was given a foot long by 3 inches thick stick. (Not so good) I explained I needed a slender one- of one inch by 8 or 10 inches, which was quickly found. Placing the stick against the first knot then tying a second knot over the stick I turned the stick to tighten the bandage (my shirt) till the bleeding stopped.

The excitement had passed and now I was freezing with no coat or shirt on, at maybe 35 degrees. So, I quickly got my shirt and coat on while we waited for the stretcher. Bringing the faller back to the landing was all that remained to be done besides a pickup ride to the hospital.

That was some training lesson I had that morning with a new batch of fallers. About 3 days later while I was at work, my wife Bonnie had a visitor from CleElum with a fresh washed t-shirt neatly ironed and folded. It was the wife of the faller who was full of praise and thanks for what I had done for her husband. Up until then Bonnie did not know what I had done, but like I told her later "thank god for a bit of Boy Scout First Aid training" he could have bled to death before he could get to a doctor.

Chapter 24

My Best Day Ever in the Woods

This was to be a very long day; I had prepared myself for it and was anxious to get started. When June rolls around it is getting late in the business of finding Spotted Owls still on their nest, so I often doubled up on the old nest sites to see in one day. This particular year the snow was slow removing itself so getting to some nest sites by road or walking were delayed. My plans were to hike into Blue Slide area off the 1000 F.S. Rd. in the early afternoon then hike out and then drive to the end of the 1207 F.S. road. After dark I would call from the road at three different nesting areas. The night calling sites were stationed perfectly; if Owls were there most likely they would answer. The reason for calling at night if the area allows for it, saves a lot of day hiking. If one gets a response from calling at night you would know what direction to travel the next day to find the animals.

The day began sometime around 10 AM; I picked up my F.S. truck at the Ranger Station and headed for White Pass. I was about 4 miles above the Oak Creek feed station on HWY 12 when six Big-Horned Mountain Sheep came charging off a steep slope onto the road just in front of me. This area had recently been stocked with Mountain Sheep by the State Game Dept. the sheep are normally high up in the hills by now, but I guess they were after water. It was a close call, but I came to a full stop, took pictures and went on my way You rarely see Big-Horned Mountain Sheep on a Highway. Here is a picture of them running back up the mountain.

Big-Horned Mountain Sheep ©Dale X Phipps

Shortly after seeing the Big-Horned Mountain Sheep I turned off HWY 12 on to Forest Service road #1200 and was headed towards the Blue Slide Northern Spotted Owl nest site on the 1000 Road. Along the way I drove around a corner in the 1000 rd. to find two calf Elk and two cow Elk running down the road in front of me. This happens a lot in the spring- animals crossing roads when a car suddenly appears-the animals keep running down the road instead of just heading back into the trees. Again, I stopped my truck and waited until the Elk came to their senses and jumped off the road.

Sometime later as I was leaving the 1000 rd. and turning onto the 129/1000 rd. I spotted a dark round coconut- like- ball in the dirt road. Slowing down and trying to drive around the odd object I could see it was the head of a new born calf Elk. Unfortunately, baby deer and elk are delicacy for Mountain Lion, Wolf, and Coyote, and what I had driven by was what was left of a predator's breakfast. This leaves an odd feeling in the back of your neck when you see that sort of thing, kind of like a winters chill.

I crossed the Bridge to Nowhere, parked my rig and gathered my gear to hike in to the Blue Slide Site, and hopefully find Spotted Owls at the Site. Bridge to Nowhere was a bridge built in advance of a Timber Sale; however, the sale was called off due to finding Spotted Owls in this area. The bridge now sits over the South Fork River of the Tieton, with an unfinished road that dead end's 200+ feet past the bridge. Wow what a delight after a two-mile hike to the nest site I found a pair of Spotted Owls with one Spud-a juvenile offspring climbing about the tree near the nest. The Spud was too high up the nest tree for me to capture and band so I will return sometime in July when the young one is closer to the ground.

Mother and baby Owls ©Dale X Phipps

After hiking back out of the trail I drove around to the 1200 road. While passing the Bear Cove Summer homes I came upon a small herd of Elk. Would you believe it-they were being chased by small yearling Bobcat? I know that he was not what started the herd running, it must have been the mother cat, but she jumped out of my sight when she heard the truck approach. It all looked cute but lasted only a minute.

By now it was starting to get dark and I had to hurry up the 1207 road to prepare to do night calling on three separate nest sites. The first at the end of the road was Scatter Creek- two spots were called there but no response. I moved on down the 1207 rd. to the Miriam Creek site, after 2 ten-minute callings no response.

Moving on to last calling area for the night and it would be Hell Creek; it was now well past 10PM which made it a prime time to call. Yes, I was right the best time to call is the latest. Right off with only a minute of calling, first a male, then a female Spotted Owl answered my calls. They were close to the road which would make them an easy find in the daylight on a return trip.

After all that, what a day! I gathered up my caller and note pad got in my rig and headed towards HWY 12. Within three miles of Hell Creek and almost to the HWY a large 7-point Bull Elk in full velvet was standing in the middle of the road and he did not like my bright lights. At first, I thought he may charge the truck, but he did not. He sauntered off the road and into the trees, leaving me a clear path to be on my way.

Once onto HWY 12 it was 55 miles an hour and I thought that was it, just homeward bound. But things were not quite over for my day-night experience. On the way down almost to the newly rebuilt Rimrock Lake Lodge on a curve to the right I spotted a fully grown Mountain Lion. I only saw him because my headlights showed his outline through low thin brush just off the road. I am sure he thought he was completely hidden behind the brush and it would have been in daylight, but my headlights totally exposed him.

Well, that is my Best Day Ever in the Forest. I have never seen that many different animals in one day in the forest before or since. Mtn. Sheep, Calf Elk, Pair of Spotted Owls and Spud, Cows and Calf Elk, Bobcat kitten, herds of Elk, a Royal Bull Elk in Velvet, and last but not least a Mountain Lion.

Mountain Lion ©Dale X Phipps

Chapter 25

Two Lost Hikers Find Me

It was late July 2014 sometime around 1500 hr. That day I had traveled most of the hillside above Soda Springs Camp Ground looking for a pair of Spotted Owls. Maybe up to 6 miles back and forth on a steep northern slope littered with wind fallen trees that I had to climb over or walk around. I had to have been with-in ½ mile from Little Bald Mountain.Lookout (which is about 2 miles straight up from Soda Springs C.G.) at one time or other in one of my passes back and forth searching and calling, but with no results finding or even hearing the Owls I had heard the night before. However, the day was getting late and I knew I was well over a mile from the Soda Springs Bridge, and my truck on the other side. The bridge was my only way back across the Bumping River at this time of year; the river was too fast and deep to cross safely without a bridge.

Then out of the blue somewhere north and west of where I had last called for the Owls, I faintly heard people talking. Now this was way out there off any trail, and I thought I was hearing things. So, I stopped to listen and sure and be dang the voices were getting closer. I waited till I could almost see them coming through the brush and trees. Then I spoke up to let them know they were not alone. And just like that I heard the woman say were safe- someone else is out here. The young man stammered I know where we are. As they approached, I asked where they were headed, and told them who I was, and a part of the Forest Service could I be of any help?

As it turned out they had camped at Soda Springs the night before and at mid-morning decided to take a hike across the Bridge and up the Little Bald Mtn.trail. Now the Trail goes West and up the mountain to the Lookout. It had taken them most of their day to get to the Lookout. Now on their way down instead of sticking with the trail the young man decided to short cut. Well due to the down fallen trees and one thing led to another they were at least ¾ of a mile way east of the trail. I told them the direction they were headed would take them to the river but over 1 ½ miles from the bridge they needed to get back to their camp.

I let them know I was on my way out and finished with my work for the day, so they were welcomed to follow me back to Soda Springs and the bridge to get us across the river safely. As I was headed down, they stayed back from me, maybe 100 ft. or so and almost out of sight. I could still hear their voices from time to time. But then no sound, so I called out to them. They answered and again they were headed too far to the East to get back on the Little Bald Mtn. trail much less find the bridge. I talked them back over to my position and said I would go slower if they needed that. His response was I thought I was back on the trail. (It was a game trail going in the wrong direction). After that the woman made sure they stuck close to me on the way to the bridge.

When we got to the Campground, they thanked me for leading them out of the forest and asked, "Do you often find lost hikers?" I told them I use to look for lost people most every summer. But no not since I retired. However, in the 35 years that I worked the Forest I have never had lost hikers find me, so I could help them find their way out. We had a chuckle over that.

What are the odds of walking into lost hikers who really don't know how badly they are lost?

ABOUT THE AUTHOR

Dale X Phipps has lived in the Yakima, Washington area since he was a small child. He spent 35 years in the United States Forest Service, Naches Ranger District, with a primary job of Timber Sale Administrator. As the Timber Sale Administrator, he participated in all phases of the job including marking trees, cruising prospective areas for consideration of sale, timber sale appraisal, and on the ground Sale Administration. Other jobs like firefighting, and rescue work are part of Forest Service employees expected duties.

In the last 2 years of his service, he assisted the Wildlife Biology team as a Technician working on the recovery of the Bull Trout in the streams and rivers of the Naches Ranger District.

In his recent retirement years, he has spent 17 years collecting field data for the recovery study of the Northern Spotted Owl on the Naches Ranger District. He assisted this endeavor by finding and mapping locations, capturing, and banding new and juvenile offspring, and preparing extensive reports on these elusive owls.

ACKNOWLEDGEMENTS

This book has taken me a long time to write. I appreciate the opportunity to have the many varied experiences that made me who I am today. I thank those who shared these times with me—my family, friends, and co-workers.

I owe special thanks to Dunk Sanger, Fred Webb, and Jim Layman who helped me learn the practical use of logging equipment in the early years.

Thanks to the management, mentors, and instructors of the United States Forest Service, Department of Agriculture for 35 years of putting up with me.

Many thanks to Ken Taylor for sharing his photographs and keeping in touch these many years.

I am grateful to Shirley A Sattler-Phipps, my wife, who believed my story was valuable and who spent numerous hours editing and proofreading to bring this book to print.

Email for Dale Phipps: boytotimberbeast@yahoo.com

City Boy to Timber Beast